# TESTIMONIALS

*"I have just finished Kat's book, and I think it's very 'spicy' and 'raw' in a good way. It goes straight to the point!*

*Everything Kat says is pretty straightfor~~~~~ it gives you a really clear 'brain set-up' that you should adopt fc facing everyday problems and other ext*

*It's Brilliant!"*

**Roberto Puddu – California, USA**

*"I only want to work with successful, strong, confident women who are c billionaires. No flip-flops, unicorn farts and hobby businesses.*

*Nah, I should qualify that: pink flip-flops and cuddle sessions.*

*The pink flip-flop brigade is banned. Kat is not the pink flip-flop brigade. Kat is 'Mrs Kick-Ass Get Shit Done Whilst Looking Amazing.'"*

**Vicky Fraser – Herefordshire, UK**

*"I have been genuinely surprised what Kat teaches about email marketing. My salon sends daily emails and what surprised me is that there were lots of new clients who were reading those emails.*

*And also men.*

*So, I asked one of my male clients whether he was reading many of my emails, and he told me that he read most of them and liked to feel part of the community. He literally said that! Also, he said that he would normally unsubscribe from most follow up emails sent by retailers, but decided to keep ours in his mailbox. So I was quite impressed with this 'backstage' process being so effective.*

*The stuff in this book really works!*

*I just have an image in my mind, I can see clients as 'planets' moving along their own 'orbits', but being a part of a bigger system."*

**Gleb Pavlov – London, UK**

# TESTIMONIALS

*Did you know that Kat bought a hair salon with zip knowledge of the hair trade? She'll tells you the full story in the book, so I'll skip the details for now.*

*My point is: the woman has balls! She isn't called the 'Queen Bitch of Everything' for nothing.*

*She dived in and made the necessary changes to her salon - and turned it around completely. From a miserable, struggling salon with pissing and moaning customers and bad cash flow, to a state-of-the-art, profitable, luxurious and successful business with well-behaving clients and customers that most entrepreneurs could only dream of.*

*Now here's the thing...*

*Most entrepreneurs who succeed in business keep their best secrets to themselves: they don't like sharing.*

*Lucky for you, Kat isn't like that. As you might know, she's sold her salon and now trains and mentors salon owners so they can replicate her results.*

*And here's the kicker: despite what 'success gurus' and 'business experts' often claim, business success actually isn't that difficult to achieve.*

*You need two ingredients:*

*The first ingredient is knowledge: you don't know what you don't know. The lack of knowledge stops many business owners from making smart decisions. I don't mean to spoil the book for you, but one of the most powerful secrets Kat reveals in her book is why you don't need to undercut your competitors to beat them.*

*The second ingredient is what really separates the wheat from the chaff: implementation. As we all know, nothing happens until something moves. To put it into plain English: this shit works if you actually put it to use for you in your own business.*

*In this book, Kat doesn't just tell you what to do and why you should do it - no - unlike most coaches and mentors, she also gives you the 'how', meaning that she actually **gives you** the step-by-step recipes for succeeding in the industry.*

*And the recipe isn't complicated at all - it's delivered in plain English and it's all clear, simple and easy to digest.*

*And last: I work directly with the industry as a supplier of software*

*Do what others want*
*Kat Smith*
*OBJE*

# *Grow* Your Salon
# FAST

The Quick, Dirty, Uncensored
Secrets to Effortless High-
Street Domination Despite
Cut-Throat Competition,
Insane Regulation and
Obnoxious Clients

KAT SMITH

*solutions. Kat's willingness to share her knowledge with me, both through her book and in our regular one-on-one mentoring sessions, has saved me from making a TON of stupid and costly mistakes.*

*If you're in the industry and are serious about what you do, this is a must-have book.*

*Follow Kat's advice, and you can't go much wrong.*

*Or don't... and watch what happens when your competitors do.*

*Your choice.*

*Want my advice?*

*Just get the damned book. Now.*

**Vegard Svanberg – Norway**

*In 2008, Kat and I found the worst salon in the best street and joined forces to start Hair Organics Notting Hill. This was my third salon and even though the first two were moderately successful, in the eighties and nineties in their own way, it was now the noughties and the UK was in the throes of a long recession, and a different approach was going to be needed to run a successful salon.*

*Without Kat, I would still be getting my head around lawyers, accountants, landlords, wages, salon computer systems, suppliers, health and safety, staff meetings, all-round quality control, and all the boring jobs that us 'creatives' hate to do.*

*And that was the easy part!*

*Now we had the presence of social media connecting with our clients before, during and after they made contact, and was deemed more important than ever.*

*Clients today have a wealth of choice, so keeping hold of them is more than just a great head of highlights or a cut and blow dry.*

*Kat took this head-on like a duck to water, and the results were amazing.*

*By the end of year one we had doubled the turnover, and given the salon a full makeover with Kat at the helm, building our brand.  By year six we had more than quadrupled our turnover and increased the staff from three to eleven.*

# TESTIMONIALS

*This was done by constant marketing through email campaigns, direct response marketing and hard work.*

*I believe Kat can drive your salon to places and turnover you would not believe.*

*Yours will be the best salon in the street.*

*And you will be doing less clients. The ones you have, will be the best ones, and your staff will respect you as they will be working in the best environment and be financially secure.*

*I can tell you this works, as I now have control of my own salon and have a life as well.*

*Kat is straight talking and to the point, so sit back and enjoy the ride.*

*You will go places!*

*I know I have, so thank you Kat Smith QBofE. Xxx*

**Terry Wilson - London, UK**


*Kat's book 'Grow Your Salon FAST' elaborates on a rule that is used in everyday life: an essential rule if you are to have a successful business - the 80/20 Principle.*

*Not only does this book give you insights on the rule but also how to apply it to your business to have more willing clients, gain extra time in a day and make more money by effectively doing less.*

*There are a lot of books out there that write meaningless jargon that:*

*A) You won't understand and...*

*B) are not even relevant to you.*

*But Kat has successfully written this book in a way that cuts through all the nonsense and simply tells you what needs to be done.*

*Finally, a one-stop-shop book that helps with all business models.*

*Thank you Kat.*

**Jaydyn Hansen – Queensland, Australia**

# CONTENTS

# Part Four - YOUR MOTIVATION - 193

# FOREWORD

I'm a hermit. I, by choice and design, live in a field in a remote and sparsely populated part of the most sparsely populated county in the sparsely populated Republic of Ireland.

And because I'm a hermit, I don't go into town too often... but when I do I see the same sad and depressing story played out time and time again... perfectly viable small businesses including and perhaps especially hair and beauty salons going out of business.

And you know the saddest thing about it all?

It's all so unnecessary.

See, the biggest secret in the salon business is it's not about how well you cut hair, paint toenails, or how well you pop or apply the countless pills and potions.

Nope. The difference between successful and unsuccessful salons is always, always about the marketing.

I know, that probably comes as a bit of a shock to you, and you probably feel rather uncomfortable right now. After all, when you started your salon you figured you'd just open your doors, do a great job of whatever it is you do, and the clients would just roll in through the door like so many wads of cash.

Right?

Right.

But you were wrong.

Chances are, you got a rush of new business and then things just settled down to where they are now. You're maybe doing 'OK' but you're not ready to buy the Rolls quite yet, and no matter how many cut-price specials you stick in the local paper or how many 'likes' and 'shares' you get on your Facebook page, nothing much seems to change.

But that's OK. There's a reason for that, and I'd be very surprised if it proved to be any different.

Fact is, you can't grow an extraordinarily successful salon by doing ordinary things. Ordinary behaviour, all other things being equal, just gets you ordinary results, (and in the business world, 'ordinary' means something like 80% of new businesses going out of business in the first five years of trading — hence my observations along my local High Street).

More to the point, copying the tediously ordinary behaviour of your fellow salon owner and competitors isn't going to get you substantially different results from the results they get either. I'd even hazard a guess you find yourself copying them on occasion, not releasing they, in their turn, are copying you. It's like the blind leading the blind. It's marketing incest, and just like with real incest, everyone gets dumber and uglier, and no-one's making any money.

So what do you do?

Another round of cut-price offers in the local paper and a flurry of posts on your Facebook page.

Pretty depressing picture I've painted there, eh?

But that's the bad news.

The good — no, great — news is that's all in the past.

It stops right here and now.

Why?

Because you hold in your hands the answer to your prayers. I promise, if you heed what Kat shares with you in these pages and take action, then your life and salon will change out of all recognition within 90 days.

No, it won't be easy. And it'll mean doing virtually everything in the way you run, market, and present your salon very differently from how you're doing it now (and very differently from how anyone else in your town is doing it too — probably the hardest thing of all to deal with).

And so I warn you: what Kat shares with you in Grow Your Salon FAST will leave you feeling very uncomfortable. You will feel tempted to throw the book across the room and shout and swear at her, and ignore the message she's giving you completely.

Do that, and you're making a huge mistake.

Because she's right in everything she says about how to grow your salon fast (and it's not fluff or theory — Kat has done this for real in the harsh and unforgiving world of the real salon business. She walks her talk and she knows her shit).

And the best news of all?

Probably 95 of every 100 people who read this book will ignore it completely.

They'll invent all manner of excuses to convince themselves the pain of change isn't worth the potential reward. They'll justify with irrelevant and flawed logic that the tried, tested, and proven tips, tactics, strategies, and techniques Kat puts in your hands won't work for them. (Because they'll all say to themselves, "my business is different.")

But if you'll be one of the smart and savvy %, gird your loins, stare the harsh reality of the salon business in the eye and do what's necessary, then you will reap the rewards.

Jon McCulloch
*The Evil Bald Genius*
www.jonmcculloch.com

# INTRODUCTION

First of all, congratulations for choosing to be in this industry – it's an ideal one for so many of the marketing tips that I'm going to be sharing with you in this book. And it is the perfect model for continuity, niching, scaling and duplicating. But don't worry I'll explain what I mean by all of that as we go along. In fact, it is one of the few business models that is, so you're already in a pretty good place. Even if you did absolutely nothing to grow your business further, you could probably support a single owner/operated salon, or a mobile salon set up. And let's admit it, there are quite a few out there.

But you are looking for more, you are craving financial freedom, you're looking to grow your salon so that it supports you without the hard-grind, the long anti-social hours, and the worry of a fluctuating cash flow. It's not enough for you to be just scraping by, or just being average, or even just surviving. You know there is more to it than what you are already doing and you want it. By the time you've finished reading this book and put the strategies into place, your business is going to be far in advance of that single owner/operated salon, or any cut-throat competitor you may once have feared.

Before we get into all that, who am I, and what am I going to do for you? Well, I'm Kat Smith, aka Queen Bitch of Everything or QBofE for short (more about why they call me that later), and in these pages I am going to take you on a ride that will at the very least make you uncomfortable. At best it will blow your mind completely. I promise to share concepts and ideas with you that will work in your business. This won't just be the good stuff; it will be the bad stuff, the ugly stuff, and everything in between. It will be your job to make sure that you understand the concepts and put them into place in order to ensure your business's success. Yes, I'm talking about doing some work already but don't fear, this stuff can be fun and when you see the results it's more than addictive.

> When you do put what you've learnt into practice, you will make more money with less work, less hassle and fewer headaches.

Well, that's why you picked up this book, right?

The thing is, I have been in your shoes and I know that what you are feeling now is frustration. You know there is something more out there, something that will give you the opportunity to make more money ethically, morally and legally. But the process of 'how to' is eluding you. I know you will have received multiple emails or phone calls from so-called 'marketers' who want you to subscribe to their 'one best way', and you may have been tempted by their offers in the past. You were given the 'what you should do' and the 'why you should do it', but not the 'how to' steps that actually make the money. (You may have also been sold snake oil, unicorn farts and dragon jizz from the unscrupulous fucktrumpets who are rife in my industry, but that will stop once you've learnt what's in these pages.)

I've been there and I know there is more to growing your business than engaging your clients on social media - a whole lot more. And this whole lot more I'm speaking of actually works. I'll give you some ideas that you can implement straight away in order to make money. Others require time to implement, test, measure and tweak before any results will be visible. I will give you the processes of exactly how to do it, so you are not just throwing shit at the wall and hoping that some of it sticks.

The concepts in this book work because they have been tried, tested and proven to succeed by me and other business owners with whom I've worked closely. For just over six years I owned a

6-chair hairdressing salon in the heart of Notting Hill, London, UK. I had a business partner, Terry, who was the brawn of the operation, running the day-to-day business and being on the floor, while I was the brains.

I am not a hairdresser by the way, I leave that to the experts. But the thing I did do was to take that business from a failing salon with a turnover of under £90K and a loss of £9K a year when I bought it (in a recession I might add), to a successful, busy salon with a turnover of close to £400K, making £77K in pre-tax profit in the 6th year. And when I sold out of it, it was worth 26 times what I had bought it for. There was no magic to this, just hard work and the implementation of the strategies that I'm about to share with you in this book.

Will it work for you? There is no reason to trust me or take my word for any of this. There are many charlatans out there who talk a good talk, but the people I allow into my Inner Circle are getting results by doing exactly what I share. And the results they are getting are staggering. But I am not trying to get you to join, we don't know each other yet, and it's by invitation only so I'm not even going to share the URL with you now.

What I want you to do is read what I have to say and test it for yourself. Don't be another spoon-fed moron who just goes along with things for an easy life. Be skeptical and cynical about what I tell you, put your critical thinking cap on and then test it all for yourself in your own business. Then you can tell me if anything I have said in this book is incorrect. Not wrong, mind. I am happy to be corrected with the actual truth. The things in this book will grow your profits substantially, and they will change your business and your life, but only if you take action.

I will say it again, there is no magic spell, no silver bullet, no 'one thing' that is going to change your business overnight. It will take work and will involve both successes and failures. If you believe otherwise you are reading the wrong book. Put it down now, package it up and send it back to me for a full refund.

**Here are some notes to clear things up at the start:**

1. **This book is for growing your salon FAST**. And by salon I mean any type of salon - hair, beauty, spa, or any combination of the three. In fact, you can take all of this book and the strategies within it and apply it to any business...any business at all. All businesses run along the same principles. The thing is, I owned a hairdressing salon with Terry for more than six years, and so it's from this experience that I've taken my real life examples. If you have a beauty salon without hairdressing and I say 'hair', simply substitute this word for 'nails' or 'skin', or whatever is relevant to you. If I say 'blowdries', substitute this word for 'manicure' or 'facials', etc. If you sell farming equipment and you picked up this book because you thought the cover was sexy, you have good taste, but substitute 'hair' for 'tractor', or whatever your implement of choice might be. You get the picture. DO NOT write to me and say that hair salons are different from beauty salons when it comes to marketing - they aren't.

2. **The beauty of the English language is that it is complex and there are many exceptions to rules, but it also has no gender-neutral, third person singular pronouns.** I'm generally lazy and think the 'he/she' debate is bullshit, so I've used just 'he' or 'she' throughout. They are interchangeable so you do the work, and no, there's no point being offended, I really don't care. Also this book has no borders when I am talking about money or prices. So unless specified just insert your denomination of choice, £, $, €, ¥, whatever floats your boat.

3. **I swear a lot**...I don't know whether that's because I come from a country (New Zealand) that features cursing on radio and TV (one famous TV ad has just the word 'bugger' repeated over and over), or whether it's because I currently live in a country where you can potentially be arrested for swearing, and because I'm perverse, that makes me want to be even more potty-mouthed. Regardless, many swear words

drop like sweet raindrops into my conversations, and, as I write like I speak, they have ended up in this book. Again, do not write to me and say that you've been offended by my language, I really don't care. And you'll end up being mocked in my daily emails and make yourself look stupid.

4. **I'm not interested in your 'feedback'.** Your unsolicited opinion about how I run my business, or how I communicate, is just that: unsolicited and just your opinion. Don't bother sending it to me unless I have written something objectively incorrect. Your opinion is irrelevant. Opinions are like arseholes, everyone has one but no one wants one waved around in their face. If you want more validation on how your feedback is irrelevant, Howard Stern puts it nicely for me in his audio clip which you can listen to here: https://katsmith.leadpages.co/feedback/

P.S. Why do they call me the Queen Bitch of Everything?

Because I am.

Well in a salon filled with 'queens' I had to position myself as the true Queen.

Bitch?

Absolutely, but only because I demand excellence. And I refuse to be responsible for other people's problems, am very comfortable with my own self for company, and am very straight talking. Why this gets people going I have no idea. I've been called intimidating, but if that is what you find offensive then that says more about your emotional response to your own beliefs than my actions.

Whatever.

Everything?

I'm a polymath, one of those annoying people who knows something about everything, mostly because I like to know how things work and why.

Enough about me, this book is about you.

# CHAPTER ONE

# GROW YOUR SALON FAST

*'Grow Your Salon FAST'* is split into the three tenets of Direct Response Marketing (DRM): – *Your Market, The Medium*, and *Your Message*, and a fourth section that you will need to get stuck into to grow your business, *Your Motivation*.

*Your Market* deals with the strategy of growing your business whereas *The Medium* deals with tactics. If you were going to focus on the most important part, in true 80/20 style (more of that later), I would advise you to eat and sleep the strategy section until you can recite it in your slumber and have a deep understanding about what marketing your business to grow it fast and make more money really involves.

There are many people in my grubby industry of Direct Response Marketing that sell you nothing but tactics, or rather they sell you fear that if you are not using the latest tactic you will not succeed in business. These people are snake oil sellers. The thing is, if you don't have an understanding of what your marketing strategy is, or you don't have the components in place, then it doesn't matter what tactic you choose to market your business, you will have limited or even no success. So it will be an expensive dabble at best, or a super-expensive bomb at worst. And you will wonder why.

The strategy is what makes your business profitable through enabling it to be replicable, scalable and measurable.

Tactics come next and can change without notice over time and at the whim of trends, and are beyond your influence. They are important in as much as they are the tools you will use to market your business. They are many and varied and some work more effectively in some markets than others and/or may suit different demographics, geographical locations and even time zones. But there will be things in this book that will work very well for you if you just try them.

Selling your product or service is all about the message you are going to send out to your prospective client. This message needs to be ethical and it needs to educate your client so that they will see that you are going to meet their wants and desires. Your message may be different to different segments of your client base, but the principles will be the same.

Human nature is such that we are all susceptible to psychological influences (and I want to stress that I only use influence to sell in an ethical manner, there is no benefit to me being dishonest or fraudulent or preying on the gullible). I always work in my own best interests, which is why you can trust me. My best interest is to attract you as a client and retain you as one. I can only do this if what I give is of value to you. It is in my best interest therefore to give you the facts of what works and to show you how so that you benefit from them and become successful. As a result I benefit from your success. So yep, I definitely want to work in my best interest.

If you are into conning people to get them in the door then this book is not for you. The majority of salon owners I speak to say they know they need to do something but they just don't know where to start. That's where *Putting It All Together* comes in. This demystifies the process and gives you a kick-start towards starting something, anything, which will get you out of the rut you are currently in.

You can thank me later.

And you will.

I've also included chapter summaries so that you can skip ahead and still get the gist of the chapter, or look back and find something you need to reread. At the end of each summary there is an action point; something that you can complete straightaway to kickstart your new marketing system. By the end of the book you should be up and running.

## A note on Creatives

You may be a creative, or you may like to think of yourself as a creative. You also may use the excuse that you can't do any of the 'business side' of things because you are a creative and therefore somewhat exempt from the real world and are one of life's precious snowflakes or special flowers. Well, that's great, the world needs creatives, and we need good artists to make our hair, nails and skin so beautiful that they are works of art in themselves. After all, hair and beauty is an art as well as a craft.

But if you think that creativity alone is going to pull people through your door, or that a pavement sign or a window poster with an artistic headshot is going to have clients stampeding your way, please close this book, put it in an envelope and post it back to me immediately. I will refund you in full.

> Creativity is what will help you keep clients coming back to you - to a point - but relentless marketing is what is going to make your business successful.

And that goes for both attracting and keeping the right clients.

Creativity gets overplayed in this industry and is purported to be the be all and end all of good business. You only have to look at the competitions that feature in trade journals. The majority of them are for creativity. Well, who exactly are you selling to? Are you selling to 'The Industry', or to real life clients who generally want one thing - to look and feel good and to hell with your creativity? But there is no point sitting in the corner sucking your thumb and rocking back and forth over it. That's not going to get shit done. The cold hard fact is that most creatives who take the route of relying on their artistry, believing that they are owed success and recognition just because it should be this way, will die poor and frustrated.

To really get results you will need to have a business head, or at least be willing to learn how to get one. The facts aren't going to lie down and go away just because you can't cope with the thought of it.

There is only one purpose of this book: To *Grow Your Salon FAST.* That is all. I've written it for that very purpose and that's what it's intended to do for you. It's not an ego-trip, a bit of light fluff or a soporific bedtime read, it's a work horse that you can read and put into action to dramatically increase your profits - all ethically, morally, legally and entirely above board.

What I want you to know is that at times you are going to feel uncomfortable, or even offended by what I tell you. What happens then is that you'll either get fearful and ignore the message and won't act on it, or you'll get angry and start to hate the messenger. I really can't stress enough how much of a shit I don't give if something I say offends you. Just be aware that this will be an emotional reaction to something I've said that you'll want me to deal with for you. Well, get over it. And if you do choose to ignore the message, that would be a shame as it's totally up to you to take the truth and succeed with it.

Or maybe you will allow your business to end up like the 80% of others that go bust within the first five years. Don't go thinking that your business is any different from the one next door, or next door to that, or the one in the next county, state or country.

The stuff in these pages works for a reason. What you have in your hand is a solid blueprint for growing your business, from lead generation to relentless follow up, which you can automate and optimise, and which will continue to grow despite recessions, the haters and the tight-arsed lenders.

## Chapter 1. Summary

→ **You are here because you are looking for more –** financial freedom and personal sovereignty.

→ **The strategies and tactics I am going to share with you work.** I have done them myself and they have been tried and tested by countless others.

→ **When it comes to marketing your business, it is no different from any other business.** Your business is not special or exempt in any way. These strategies work for any small business. You just have to do the work.

→ **You need to learn how to market your salon.** Put aside your creativity and embrace the fact that you have to be a business-driven salon owner.

→ **If you are a special snowflake or sensitive flower then this book is not for you.**

→ **You are holding a blueprint for growing your business in your hand.**

### Take Action

Write down your current strategy for getting new clients through your door and making more out of existing ones. Make the list as detailed as possible and include everything you currently do. Now keep it in a safe place, as we will come back to it later.

# *Part One*
# YOUR MARKET

# CHAPTER TWO
# WHAT IS YOUR STRATEGY?

Your overall strategy is to attract the right type of buyers, establish a relationship with them, sell them a product or service that gives them value, and then continue to sell them more of the same or something different until they die or move away (and even then you can still sell to them if they have moved - dead is a bit harder). The foundation of marketing your business is to have the right procedures in place, which are formally organised and operating continually, so that if you are not there for whatever reason, your business will continue without you and, more importantly, will continue to *make money*.

It's like a production line; stuff gets fed into the line at the start, is processed and then spat out at the end in the desired form. If you don't feed in the stuff at the start, there will be a drop in the finished product; if you mess about with the process in the middle or fail to do it in order, your product will not be what you desire; if you don't do anything with the product after it comes off the line, it lies neglected and useless on the floor.

In other words, when you are marketing your business you want to be feeding leads (people who have raised their hands and shown an interest in you) in at the start, nurturing them until they buy something from you and become a client, which is your desired outcome, and then nurturing them from there to keep them as a repeat, loyal client. This is your overall strategy, and yes it really is that simple. There are no tricks, no secrets, no quick fixes, just a lot of work to keep this cycle going.

The great thing is though, once you have your strategy in place, the results you get from the tactics you use can be phenomenal. Growth in your business will be cumulative and the profits will be exponential. I am not going to sugar coat it though;

it will be hard work. You will have a lot to learn. Learning can be frustrating, but you learnt this trade, right? You've already invested hours into learning your skill, and you're undoubtedly an expert in it. Someone who has done 10,000 hours in any field is considered an expert.

Owning and running a successful business is also a skill, and to become an expert in that you have to put in the time.

Make no mistake, this shit means work. I'm not giving you a magic formula. But stick with me and I will show you how simple some of it can be, and I'll also explain what you are doing wrong that you can stop so that you will see results straight away.

## A note about Strategy vs. Tactics

When it comes to marketing your business, there is only one thing that you need to remember: marketing is getting the right message to the right person at the right time and in the right way. And that is all. This has been the same since Og the caveman wanted to sell his stone club to Ug the caveman and sent him a sample (and a sales letter with an attention-grabbing headline, blistering copy and a strong and clear call to action) by mammoth post. And it hasn't changed since. Whether it is selling plastic surgery to recent divorcees via sales letters, rampant rabbits to the same market via email, or black eyeliner to goths via an ad in Emo Magazine, the strategy is the same. You want your message to get to your target market in a way that they will respond to, so that they will become your client and grow your business and help it become successful.

Lather, rinse, repeat.

The tactics you use, however, can be numerous and varied. A particular tactic in isolation will not grow your salon fast, no matter which unscrupulous douchebag is trying to sell you the 'one thing' or 'the secret' that will get clients through your door. Beware of the sellers of unicorn farts and fairy shit who will guarantee you unlimited clients through one medium. In general, it will most likely be a combination of tactics, and repeating them, that will get you the results.

> Tactics are the steps or processes you take to get your thing in as many of the faces of the right people who want your product or service as possible.

Advertising your thing with Facebook ads is a tactic (not to be confused with getting likes for your page). Giving referral cards to your clients to share with their friends is a tactic. Sending a sales letter with a gift inside (bulky mail) to non-returning clients inviting them back is a tactic. Are you starting to get the picture? Good. The thing about tactics is that they change with efficacy and technology and trend.

Your strategy never changes but the tactics could become obsolete. Facebook's platform could close down (unlikely? that's probably what Myspace thought), or the rules could change in the way you are allowed to advertise on Google's platform. Alternatively, the tactic you've been using could become less effective and need tweaking - clients may decide they prefer digital referral cards over printed ones. And you will have to move with the changes or lag behind at your peril.

You can't rely on one tactic to fill your salon. That is business suicide. But you also want to ensure that the tactics you are using are the right fit for your message, market and media. It's extremely helpful to use the 80/20 principle to do this (as I will talk about later), so that you are not wasting your time trying to get engagement through Facebook likes (WTF?), rather than spending time tweaking adverts on Facebook that are driving highly qualified leads to your website.

Never Forget: Fail fast, recover quickly, move on.

The great thing about focusing on your strategy and having many highly flexible tactics is that you can shift things around quickly - you can effectively pivot onto another tactic if one has failed. And yes, even the best marketers, i.e., me, have tested something that has failed. And not just failed, but failed spectacularly. I'll give you an example...

## Real Life Example

I paid a good copywriter to write a couple of sales letters to be sent out to the clients of a specific stylist who had left my employment. These specific clients hadn't come back into the salon after a 12-month period. The first sales letter I sent out was a compelling, *"was it something we said?"* missive, stating that we had missed them and wanted them back. It included a voucher for a service because *"we really think that much of you"*, and it hinted that their hair was probably missing our ministrations. The voucher was time-limited and the call to action was to phone the salon to redeem it by making a future appointment before the due date. The envelope was handwritten and a real stamp was duly licked and stuck to it (yay for juniors!). It had all the ingredients of a successful piece of marketing. It went out to 50 highly-targeted lapsed clients.

The response?

Not a dicky-bird.

Tumbleweed and a lot of wind (actually, we got a few

return to senders as our former clients had obviously moved, but that does not a returning client make). Not to worry, sometimes people don't respond to the first thing that crosses their path. Marketing, if you remember, relies on being in the face of your client at the right time. So letter number two was printed up and sent out with a gift inside: a little hairbrush that folded up into a handbag size with our logo printed on it. The letter went along the lines of: "*We sent you a letter but didn't hear from you, perhaps you would like this little gift and a reminder to use your voucher.*" I was sure this would work this time, no one can resist opening a package and our copy was sooooo compelling.

*Boom.*

We had response in spades, but not the kind of response I'd been expecting. You see, this time I had trusted my then business partner to post the little packages, and he completely fucked up the postage. So instead of the packages being delivered and the would-be client being delighted and picking up the phone, the postal service sent a slip to the recipient telling them that a package was being held at their local postal office and they would have to pay not only the deficient postage, but also a handling charge if they wanted to retrieve it.

Oh boy.

Well, the complaints came flooding in about the fact that they were made to walk, crawl, drive, fly to their postal office and pay money for something they didn't want and something they hadn't asked for - and what the hell was it anyway?

One woman even walked to the salon with the package and castigated me as she was crippled and had to walk with crutches and it was a long way to the post office, and then to the salon to say she didn't want it, and besides, she had her hair done at home now because she wasn't mobile any more, etc, etc.

Needless to say, a third letter was sent out with an apology and a cheque for the full amount of money that the postal office had charged. Not everyone cashed the cheque it must be said, and a few laughed and said they found it amusing (as I had), but we didn't get any returning clients.

This was such a disaster considering the costs involved that I wanted to try again to make sure it wasn't the post thing that had driven down the response. I sent the same letters, with the same bulky mail in the same way, to a different set of non-returning clients. I got one taker.

So I gave it up as a bad idea (or just shelved it) and concentrated on the next thing that was making me money but could be better - referral cards, but more on those later.

The good thing is that there are many, many marketing tactics out there, more than you probably think, and many of them are overlooked, so you have plenty to choose from, test and measure. Some are more effective than others and your market may respond better to some forms than others. For example, at the time of writing this, Facebook ads do better when selling business-to-clients (B2C), and LinkedIn ads do better when selling business-to-business (B2B). But that could change. There are some tactics that transcend all businesses and do really well regardless, email marketing, for example, and you would be a cockwomble if you left that out of your tactics.

All that aside, never forget your strategy: Getting good clients into your salon and keeping them there.

That is all marketing is. If you think that you don't need to do marketing, you are mistaken. Marketing is not the same thing as branding or engaging people with social media (surely one of the most vomit-inducing pastimes anyone has ever invented), it is critical to your growth as a business, and it never stops. I'll say that again, as it is that important: it never stops. It is relentless

It is also something that you can't 'not afford' to do. Forget having a marketing budget; that is something that big corporations do to pay the wages of 'marketers' who 'brainstorm' adverts that feature multi-coloured penguins telling clients that they stand out from the crowd. That is not going to help you and it is a fast and expensive road to ruin.

So here are the key things you need to know so that you can build your strategy foundation. You need to have an answer to all of these to have the whole picture:

## Know Your Market

Attracting the right type of client means knowing exactly what your market is...you need to know who your ideal client is, where they hang out, what their interests are, what they eat for breakfast, what their beliefs are, what their desires are and what brand their vibrator is. The more you know about your ideal client, the more specific you can be in your marketing; targeting those people who are more likely to want your product and service and appealing to their desires. You will also be able to repel those who don't meet the criteria, who are time-wasters or not suited to you. Not only does this give you clients that you like and want to do business with, but with clear targeting you can be more efficient and discerning about where you are putting your money to buy these clients.

## Know Your Price

Consider this: every client who comes through the door comes with some kind of cost attached. Whether that is cost from a sign in the window, cost from an advertisement on the radio, or cost from a referral strategy. There is really no such thing as getting a client free. But also consider this: most people in the industry will talk about their 'marketing budget' and set aside a specific amount of money each year to 'buy' clients, as if they were a major corporate with a marketing division.

In fact, it makes a shitload more sense to ask this question: *"What is the lifetime value of my client?"* and then use that answer to decide how much money you are prepared to spend to get them through your door. Once you've decided that, you then have a benchmark to work with and can set about reducing that price until the quality of leads dips below the lower cost of getting one. Clever.

So how do you know how much to spend on marketing and whether what you are doing now is a good return on investment? Let me put that another way: do you know what the average lifetime value of your client is? This sounds a bit strange, as each client will spend a different amount depending on their needs, but there will be an average you can work out.

Take a client who is a regular and has been with you for a number of years. How much do they spend in a year? Now, take that number and multiply it by 11 - the average time, in years, this client will stay with you (according to the statistics).

---

Say the client spends £500 per year.
That's £500 x 11 = £5500 over their lifetime.

---

How much money would you invest to get that one client into the salon? 50p? £5? £50? It starts to make sense now, doesn't it?

A classic 'marketing budget' just does not fit in the case of a small to medium-sized business (and it does my head in when I see the criteria in applications for salon industry marketing awards which ask: *"What is your marketing budget?"* like you have a department that is allocated a set amount of money and is not allowed to spend beyond that). Even at a rough guess, you can estimate your lifetime client value by dividing your annual turnover by the number of clients in the business. That will give you a fair idea of what a client is worth to you over a 12-month period.

Once you have that knowledge - and that's a simple 10-minute job, you now have the power to say, *"I'm prepared to spend £1.20 per person on a bulky mail campaign going out to highly qualified prospects, but not £575 on a quarter page advert in a glossy magazine that goes out to numerous people who may not be the right fit for my business."* The more you spend is not the answer to the more you get. Sure, you can get better quality leads sometimes by spending more money, but the idea is to get the cost of good quality clients down to a level that is giving you the best return on investment. And then the next idea is to make that happen over and over and over again so that you have an unlimited stream of the right client coming through the door.

Lather, rinse, repeat.

## Establish A Relationship

Once you have attracted your potential client and they have raised their hand and said that they are interested in learning more about your product or service, you begin a relationship with them. Think of it like this: When you are seeking pain relief for that wicked devil playing the recorder and the bass drum when you have a hangover, you know what you need and you need it fast, but buying hair and beauty services and products requires a lot of trust on the client's part.

How do they know you are the right person for the job? After all, a bad hair day after a visit to the salon is a bad hair year in their minds. A disastrous colour or cut is a nightmare of epic proportions, and nothing will convince them otherwise. So not only do you have to have the right skills for the job, you need to be giving your client something to hang their trust on. And that, my friend, is you. You and your personality, plus the information you educate them with, are the things that are going to seal the deal on whether they will step in the door, and it is the same for the ones you will repel.

## Retain And Repeat

Once your client is in the door and you have given them your expert service and they have received value from you, you'll want to retain them. Even though you can buy an endless stream of new clients with the right marketing, it is far more beneficial to sell more to existing clients. It makes more economic sense to do this and besides, going through the process of building a new relationship each time takes effort; keeping a relationship going is less time-consuming, and it can be far more rewarding. Almost to the point where you may never have to peddle for new clients again. Or very rarely.

So that is your overall strategy, nothing earth shattering there I admit, but if you get this it will make your life so much more easier and profitable. I will be going into more detail throughout this book, and will break information down into your market, your message and the medium you use to get your message to your market. But remember, the golden rule in marketing is getting the right message to the right person at the right time in the right way. And that is all.

## *Advanced Bonus: The 80/20 Principle*

I want to introduce you to a very clever man - his name is Vilfredo. Vilfredo Pareto. Signor Pareto happened to be an economist who was studying the disparity of wealth in society when he stumbled on what we now know as the '80/20 Principle', also known as the *'Law of the Vital Few'*. This happened in 1897, when Vilfredo was studying patterns of wealth and income in nineteenth-century England. In his research, he discovered that most income and wealth was possessed by a minority of people. This might seem like a no-brainer, but from here he also found two things that got his Italian juices flowing...

1. **There was a consistent mathematical relationship between the proportion of people and the amount of income or wealth they enjoyed, and that the distribution of wealth across the population was predictably unbalanced.**

2. **The pattern of imbalance was repeated consistently when he looked at the data across different time periods or in different countries.** The same pattern repeated itself over and over again.

What this means in English is there was a pattern of a small proportion of people having the most wealth, where the bulk of the population had less than average means. And it wasn't just in his area. The phenomenon occurred across the world. And still does.

Sadly, although Vilfredo was a great economist/mathematician, he wasn't very good at communicating his ideas, and it took a while for anyone to really use the 80/20 Principle and explain the phenomenon and its implications. We can't deny the 80/20 Principle exists. The 80/20 Principle means that in any system, the majority of effects come from a small number of causes.

Vilfredo found that 80% of wealth was owned by just 20% of people. And funnily enough, a century later this still holds true. But it's not all about the distribution of wealth, although that's an interesting topic in itself.

**The principle holds true in all other areas of life:**

- In software, just 20% of functions are used 80% of the time.
- Just 20% of your carpets get 80% of the wear.

- 80% of people live in 20% of the towns.
- 80% of people die of 20% of the most common causes.
- 80% of crime is caused by just 20% of criminals.
- On Facebook, you'll do 80% of your interaction with just 20% of your friends.
- In your wardrobe, just 20% of your clothes will be worn 80% of the time.

And so on…

Once you understand the pattern you will start to see this everywhere. 20% of the colours you use in the salon will be used 80% of the time. 20% of your staff will bring in 80% of your turnover.

The numbers don't have to be 80 and 20. They can be 90/10, 99/1, and so on. And although it isn't fair, you can't change the numbers, you can only make choices about what you want to do in the face of them, and how you can use them to your advantage.

Here's the exciting thing about this principle and why I am making such a big deal about it: If you took this single principle and invested all of your time and energy into putting it into practice, your life, and your business, would be transformed beyond anything you imagined possible, and all the rest would just be the cherries on top.

For you, as a salon owner, the relevance is about to become clear. Take the 80/20 Principle and apply it to your salon.

**I will guarantee you will find:**

- 80% of your business comes from just 20% of your clients.
- 80% of your sales are for just 20% of your products or services.
- 80% of your profits come from sales of just 20% of your products and services (and they aren't necessarily the same as the ones above).

- 80% of your marketing results come from just 20% of the marketing you do.
- 80% of your headaches, stress and problems come from just 20% of your clients.
- 80% of your achievements come from just 20% of the time you spend working on them.

What does this tell you about your business currently?

80% of your time is effectively wasted.

Oh shit.

But perhaps you already know that and had a nagging voice in the back of your head saying something was not quite right, or not quite working the way it should.

**Fear not, here's where the Principle can help you:**

Your most effective and profitable 'things' are 16 times as effective and profitable as your least effective things. Here's why: If you have 100 tasks of equal difficulty to do and 100 hours to do them in then...

1. **The 80/20 Principle means you will do 80 of them in just 20 hours.** That means you're getting four tasks done every hour when you're at your most productive. (80 tasks ÷ 20 hours = 4 tasks per hour.)

2. **80/20 also means you'll do the remaining 20 tasks in 80 hours.** And that means you're taking four hours for each task.

In other words, in the time it takes you to carry out your least productive tasks - four hours - you could have carried out sixteen of your most productive ones, because you can do four of those every hour.

Is the penny dropping? I hope so. The information I've just given you is so profound that it should change the way you do business forever. It should also change your life, giving you more insight into what is important and what is not. This will give you freedom, but only if you act on it.

**For example you should:**

- ✓ **Focus your efforts on the clients who are worth the most to you.** If these are also your favourite clients, it's no big surprise and a bonus to boot. If they are not your favourite clients, you need to change this so that you're doing your most productive work with the people you like to work with.

- ✓ **Identify the tasks within your business that yield the best results and do more of them.** Stuff that is not giving you results should be delegated, relegated, automated, or just ignored. Your mantra should be *"Delegate, Outsource, Automate."*

- ✓ **Take the time you save by delegating, etc., and invest it on high priority tasks.** A common mistake is to waste the time you save and treat it as 'free time'. Don't. Take that time to do more of the important stuff.

- ✓ **Embrace the idea of recursion.** Take your business as a whole and you will find that the 80/20 relationship runs all through it. Take the top 20% of something and you'll find that there is an 80/20 split within that. Take the top 20% of that and you'll find another 80/20 split, and so on. This means that in a clientele of say 1000, 200 of them are great clients, 40 of them are excellent clients, eight of them are outstanding clients, and at least one of them is going to be truly and unbelievably awesome.

- ✓ **Grow a pair (or strap on a pair, whatever your persuasion) and fire your worst 20% of clients.** Take no prisoners – these people are energy vampires and will suck the life out of you. I'll give you an example of how to do this later in the book. (Works with staff too...)

- ✔ **And here's a challenge for you:** Grow an even bigger pair and fire *all but* your top 20% of clients...

## Chapter 2. Summary

→ **Marketing is getting the right message to the right person at the right time through the right medium.**

→ **Your strategy is to attract the right type of buyers, establish a relationship, sell them something of value, and then continue to do so.**

→ **Strategy is your overview of making your business successful.** Tactics are the steps you take to get your message in front of your prospect.

→ **The 80/20 Principle or *'Law of the Vital Few'* explains how all systems work...the majority of effects come from a small number of causes.**

→ **Use the 80/20 Principle to work out where best to focus your efforts to build your business and make more money.**

### Take Action

Pull together your figures for the last two to three years and work out your client average lifetime value.

# CHAPTER THREE

# WHO IS YOUR IDEAL CLIENT?

You can't be all things to all people. When asked the question, *"Who is your ideal client?"* do you answer, *"anyone with a credit card"?* I remember an interview I had for a part-time marketing position with an aeronautical manufacturer very many years ago. One of the questions was, *"who is a client?"* The answer that usually came out of people's mouths, and the one that was expected, was, *"the people who want to buy aeroplane parts"*. Of course, I was a bit smarter than that and said: *"Everyone is a potential client. You can promote the company wherever you are. Clients come from referrals and from friends and acquaintances. Nobody is not a client."* I tried hard to keep the smirk off my face as the interviewer looked impressed and I got the job.

But I was wrong.

But only half wrong, and I'll come back to that later.

The thing is, a client with a credit card can be a liability. Especially if that card is stolen, or, as happened in my salon, when the person with the card (in this case the boyfriend of a new client who rang to pay for his girlfriend's full head of highlights) turns out to be shifty. The receptionist had thought it was really sweet that this guy was treating his partner. Sweet little shit. The credit card was declined when the receptionist put it through, but only after the girlfriend had left the salon. And of course, there was never any answer on the phone number he gave. (There's a big lesson there regarding having processes in place so this sort of thing doesn't happen - read the section on processes in *Relentless Follow up* and implement it as fast as you can to stop money walking out the door.)

Regarding my statement in the interview about everybody being a potential client, well, there is no such thing. If you appeal to everyone you will be wasting a whole lot of time not targeting clients who are your best fit.

Unsurprisingly, the 80/20 rule comes into play here, plus my favourite game, '*Would you rather...*'

## Would you rather...

Have a small number of loyal clients who will buy absolutely everything from you, do exactly what you ask them to do, achieve great results because they use the products you recommend, and with whom you love to deal?

*Or...*

Thousands of one-off clients that piss and moan about the price, damage their hair and skin using crap products, expect you to fix other people's mistakes and take you for a ride?

Pick one.

I don't need to tell you that it's far more satisfying to deal with people you know and like than having to put the effort into new relationships with the next walk-in who thinks you owe them a solution to their self-inflicted problems. And your lovely, loyal clients will talk about you in reverential tones, and refer you to others who are just like them.

Can you see where I am going here? A clientele of people who are similar to you and whom you like, will be a pleasure to deal with. Your days spent in your salon just got a whole lot better. It's more fun too - you'll want to go to work (and your staff will too). The best way to get staff to turn up for work is to create a place they want to come to. Putting all the staff management and incentive bullshit aside, if your staff are having to deal with shitty clients, ones that make life miserable with price buying, complaints, whines and moans, why would they want to come to work? On the other hand, if they have a column of clients they look forward to each day, all the extra stuff is just a bonus.

You're welcome.

## Create An Avatar Of Your Ideal Client

When I sat down to write this book, I had (and still have) one person in mind. My ultimate ideal client. And if you are still reading this book then it's you. But when I am writing or thinking about the products I can create in my business, I am also targeting one ideal client. This is the client I want to do business with. The client I would walk over coals for, because they are my raison d'etre. And although I have that person in my head and can describe their attributes, values and even their thoughts perfectly and without hesitation, I had to start by creating an Avatar.

An Avatar has the look, feel, likes, dislikes, personality and characteristics of your ideal client. It may be that your ideal client is a mix of many of the clients you already have. But they have the ideal characteristics of each, and they become the ultimate client... someone you want to deal with every single day. It's highly likely that they will be someone just like you. Mine is.

You see, we do business with people we like, and we like people who are like ourselves.

It's one of the laws of influence. Robert Cialdini goes into great detail about this in his book *'Influence: The Psychology of Persuasion.'* We are more compliant with people we like and we cooperate more when people's values are in line with our own, which is why celebrity sells and why 'good cop, bad cop' works. If you want to know more, I highly recommend reading this book.

My Avatar for my ideal client could be either male or female, and is probably both. She exists solely for my benefit and the characteristics on the next page, are not finite. She is constantly evolving as I develop my business. As an aside, when I wrote these Avatars, I didn't deliberately write the ideal client as a female and the client I would repel as a male (or did I?), it's just a coincidence. Sam could just as easily be a he, and Chris a she.

### Meet Sam

Sam is a salon owner. She has owned her salon for a number of years and is not always on the floor; she takes time away from her business to try and figure out how to make it successful. Sam is between 35 and 55 and is probably married and has a family. She is a homeowner and probably has an investment property too. She is a libertarian (although probably is not aware of it).

She's an entrepreneur and is competitive and ambitious. She is concerned that she doesn't know enough about how to market her business, but at the same time she doesn't know where to get the right information from, and, more importantly, whom she can trust.

She likes quality. She shops at high-end stores and likes luxury products when she sees that she is getting value. She tries to set a good example for her kids and be a role model for them. She's not afraid of hard work and will muck in and get her hands dirty if that's what's required, but more to learn about how it's done, find a way to make it more effective and efficient and then teach it to someone else.

She is a reader and reads about many subjects avidly. She likes being sold to, when the selling is seductive and well done. She appreciates that people in business are there to make a living and there is no harm or stigma in wanting to do well. Sam likes fine things and will hold out for the perfect thing, even if it means no instant gratification. She's supportive of her partner, and although she recognises that she is part of a team, she asserts that she is an individual in her own right. Her time is just as precious, her needs and wants just as important, and she makes that clear.

When it comes to business, Sam wants to do well. No, she wants to do more than well. She is not satisfied with mediocre results and is willing to listen to and model herself on successful business owners. She takes a scientific approach to business, like most things in her life, and is willing to test, measure and improve. She is willing to invest time and money into getting it right.

Sam has metaphorical balls. Big ones. She feels the fear and jumps in anyway. When things go wrong, she lives by a policy of a no blame culture. She feels responsible for the things she does and the consequences of her actions. She is not looking for a fix from the government, other people, rights groups, or the collective universe in general. She knows that life is short, you were born alone and you will die alone, and once you are dead you are dead. What you do in the meantime is your legacy so she wants to get on with it. Oh, and she loves cats.

Sam is the client you will love to deal with. She will take your recommendations and run with them. And the results she will get will reflect on your skill and it will be like a big old love in. Neither of you will be able to get enough.

As you can see, you can have fun with this, and the more you drill down to your perfect client, the more strategic you can get with marketing to this person. You can tailor your copy, advertising and website to that exact individual, which will resonate with them so that they will want to know more about your product and what it can do for them. It will also very effectively filter out all the other thousands of flotsam and jetsam that you don't want to deal with.

> If you get this right, one of the things that keep you awake at night, i.e., client complaints, will suddenly and not so magically fall away.

Dealing with clients who like you and with whom you like to deal will reduce complaints exponentially.

Shitty clients who enjoy a moan are no longer being serviced by you, so when a complaint does rear its head, you know there's a pretty genuine reason, which can probably be resolved without the resulting stress.

### Meet Chris

Chris is the opposite of Sam in almost every way. He is also a business owner, but he thinks that the world owes him a favour. Chris is cheap and desperate and wastes a lot of time and effort trying to get the best deal or things for free. Even if the quality is poor. Chris knows it all and even if he signs up for information to grow his business (usually moving from free offer and download to free offer and download), he will never act on it. Rather, he will continue to blame the economy, the government, the seasons, school holidays, tourists, etc., for his lack of business growth.

He sees selling as 'dirty' and is more focused on image and branding than using marketing techniques that show a clear and measurable return on investment. Chris is also an askhole - someone who asks the same question repeatedly and expects to get a different answer each time. Chris leans to the left or the right when it suits him, and if he wants to please his friends. He's all for freedom of speech, except when it goes against his values and opinions or hurts his feelings.

He believes that people are entitled to live their own lives unless they are doing something he finds a bit yucky, like rough sex, even when it's consensual, and then he will want it banned. Chris believes in an omnipresent Sky Daddy, because that's what his family before him has done, and it's nice to stick with tradition. Don't get him wrong, he appreciates everyone's views and is tolerant of other religions and beliefs and practices, just as long as it doesn't conflict with his own true beliefs.

Chris is one of those people who spends a lot of time following the trends of social media and thinks it's more important to get people 'engaged' in his business by collecting likes and posting artistic photos than actually learning how to advertise his business to his ideal client. When Chris is shown a sound marketing tactic that gets results but requires hard work, or makes him feel uncomfortable, he will tell you that it wouldn't work in his business as his business is unique and 'special', and he won't even bother to test it. Chris is complacent, but can't work out why the flow of money is heavily in the out direction of his business.

Chris is a dick. And if you let him in, watch him become the client from hell. Now, these are examples of my ideal and not so ideal Avatars. You can create your own to fit within your own business – yes, Chris, you can, it works for everyone.

## Real Life Example

Here is an example of the Avatar we created for my salon:

### Introducing Amy...

Age: 37-47 years old.

Has a child or two.

Is married or in a long-term relationship.

Is a senior businesswoman. She knows her profession very well and has worked up the ranks to be a leader and expert in what she does.

Earns 90k – 250k per year.

Wears high-end, branded clothing but only a few key pieces, which she mixes with high-street brands. The high-end brands are not flashy or well-known; they are high quality and unique. You will only know that they are expensive if you are 'in the know'.

She is independent from her partner, contributes equally to household expenses and has her own interests outside the home.

She likes to cook, owns a lot of cookbooks, but doesn't spend a huge amount of time in the kitchen. She likes to buy organic foods when possible and tries to cook balanced and nutritious meals for her family.

She shops at Waitrose.

Her house is homely and comforting but is also peppered with unique pieces of art and knickknacks collected from her travels. She loves travelling, not just to the usual tourist hotspots, but also to places that are unique. She loves to teach her kids about new cultures and delights in new experiences.

Time is a very precious commodity to her as she is always busy with her work, her kids and her partner, parents and friends. She gets very little time to indulge in herself so when she finds that time she is not always comfortable as she feels she should be doing something for someone else. It takes a while for her to relax into the indulgence of being pampered. She knows afterwards that she feels so great and refreshed that she should do it more often, but the guilt is always there.

She doesn't necessarily subscribe to glossy magazines or newspapers, but her guilty pleasure is reading gossip magazines.

She likes to dine out, but not at well-advertised places. She prefers to find unusual and unique boutique restaurants that provide something different.

She gets bored easily and likes to explore new things.

She cares about her health and knows that she is aging and that certain things have changed for her, especially in her body after children. She is an advocate of healthy eating and she is pretty regular with exercise. She is confident in her looks and really doesn't care anymore what other people think of her.

She cares about her children's health and the health of her partner – he is aging like her and aware of his mortality too. She knows how much her children, her partner and her parents rely on her so she needs to stay well and healthy.

She loves the cinema or any entertainment that provides escapism. She doesn't get to do it often enough.

She has a small circle of very best girlfriends and has been friends with them for a long time. They know each other well and can call on each other for favours and helping out. But mostly she is independent and 'handles' everything on her own.

See? It's easy. (It's also a great way to get staff involved in the business, helping them to understand from the outset, what your marketing strategy is and why you are doing it. 'Amy' was printed out and pinned to the back room noticeboard so my staff could refer to it often.) The more time you spend on this in the beginning, the clearer the picture of your ideal client will be, and you can then be very specific in your marketing. You will then be able to tailor your products and services accordingly. This takes out the scattergun approach of figuring out what your client wants, allowing you to focus on getting the product or service bang on so that they keep coming back for more.

At the same time, you are actively repelling the type of person you don't want coming through the door. And the way to maximise this is through *Polarisation* and *Premier Positioning*.

## Chapter 3. Summary

→ **Your Ideal Client is not everyone who walks through the door.**

→ **It is much easier to work with clients you like and who are like you:** it makes having a salon business far more pleasurable.

→ **Creating a Client Avatar helps you identify your Ideal Client and allows you to tailor your marketing directly to them.**

→ **Your team will also have a better understanding of the type of person you want to attract if you have a Client Avatar.**

→ **Attract your Ideal Client and repel your Client from Hell.**

### Take Action

Given the examples in this chapter, take some time out of your business and write up your Ideal Client and Client from Hell Avatars. Be as detailed as you can. Share them with your team and put them in the staff room. Refer back to them frequently to tailor your services, products and marketing.

CHAPTER FOUR

# PREMIER POSITIONING – WHO ARE YOU AND WHAT DO YOU STAND FOR?

You've had a dream, you've gone into business and you've slaved hard. You've worried about how to pay the bills, you've dealt with nightmare staff, you've battled with the landlord for the right to play music during the day. No one is going to tell you how you should run your business.

Are they?

Many businesses fail because they allow their clients, the public, their well-meaning friends and their even more well-meaning family to tell them who they should let through the door.

---

But take special note: If you want your business to be successful it's your business, your rules.

---

That is the crux of *Premier Positioning* or how you orientate yourself, your image, your behaviour and the messages you give out about yourself. Once you set your rules, you need to position yourself and your business so that your clients know your rules.

Here's the thing, and it's not hard, you have a choice. People will treat you the way you allow them to. If you are a 5000-dollar escort who only takes appointments from a pre-qualified list, you are not going to get the chav who is walking past the street corner. Everyone who comes into your business does so by your invitation.

You get to choose whether to deal with low-end or high-end clients. You get to choose what type of clients they are. You get to choose when and how you deal with them. What you don't get to choose is the consequences of those choices.

For example, if you choose to take a client at 6.55pm when you shut the doors at 7pm, that tells them that you will always take them for a late appointment and go past your closing time. Or if you choose to give a one-off credit instead of taking an upfront cash payment, you are telling the client this will be acceptable next time, and the time after that, and so on. They will always take advantage of that, but only because you let them.

You might do what you do because everybody else out there does, and you think you need to compete with them. But forget what your competitors are doing. Most businesses engage in 'me too' marketing, which is the surefire way to an early grave or a trip to the asylum. Any business or salon owner that positions themselves in any meaningful way immediately makes a powerful statement of differentiation.

> Once you start marketing with your own personality, differentiating yourself from the other 'me too' morons, you will typically both attract and repel clients.

The clients you will attract will be the ones you want to have in your business, and you will get more pleasure from them and have better business success because of it.

You also have a choice of the market within the industry. If you choose to deal only with high-end clients, selling a high-end service and products, you are naturally going to position yourself as a high-end salon owner, and all that implies. If you choose to sell to lower-end price buyers, your positioning will also be reflected as low-end.

Premier Positioning is two-fold: being seen as an expert, and being seen as someone worthy of respect. These two areas do often overlap, but you can easily be one without the other. I am sure we can all think of experts we think are utter cockwombles, and people we respect greatly who are experts in nothing at all.

Premier Positioning is also directly linked to Premium Pricing, which I go into in the following chapter. There is a symbiotic relationship between how you position yourself and the prices you charge, so some of the information below is interlinked, but it will make more sense once you see the two as working together.

**There are five distinct parts to Premier Positioning:**

1. Inner Game
2. Expert Status
3. Alpha Positioning
4. Powerful Differentiation
5. Polarisation

Over the next few pages I will go into more depth about each of these areas, and how you can use them.

## The Inner Game

This may sound all airy-fairy and tree-huggery, but as I don't do that type of shit it's not. But the inner game in Premier Positioning is often the hardest thing for people to grasp, and it's even harder to do.

The underlying principle is that you decide your own worth and you don't need permission or approval for the rules you make for your own business. It's your business, your positioning - nobody gets to decide how it works except for you. You are also not obliged to take responsibility for other people's problems. So if they don't like your prices, or how you run your business, you have to let them go.

It's counterintuitive to most people, and very few will do it, but if you are still with me decide what are you worth, what your time is worth, or what your products or services are worth. If you don't value yourself, you probably don't value your products or services and your prices will reflect this. I think there is an external force driving this belief system in the industry you are in as well. For many, going into the salon or beauty industry is seen as a 'vocational' option, for people who are not academically inclined. But what the public fails to realise is the level of skills required to do what you do.

It's not for everyone.

You know that skilled employees have worked hard, undergone hours of training in academies and schools and on the floor. And someone can be a skilled technician but it takes a certain amount of talent to be the master. if you are looking for self-worth just think about the fact that no one else can make a client feel as good about themselves as you do in an hour. Not a therapist, not a personal trainer, not a priest. You need to get over the hang-up of 'just a hairdresser' or 'just a beautician'; adding *Premier Positioning* and *Inner Game* helps you do this.

In a practical sense, if you decided to go high-end, your inner game changes, and there is nothing better than someone saying, *"I'm not paying that price"* and you telling them to *"fuck off!"*

## Expert Status

Premier Positioning implies expert status.

If you don't feel worthy, you are going to find it very hard to pass yourself off as an expert. And an expert is what you want to be in your area. Although if you can't talk on your subject for at least an hour then you are not an expert, so put this book down now and go and learn a bit more about it. But once you start working with quality people, who want to be dealing with you and want your value, you will start feeling more like you deserve it.

Just the fact that you increase your prices and sell your product or service on the value of it, will increase your confidence and make you feel better about yourself. Funny how these things work, but if you are seen as an expert, your perceived worth increases. No one expects world-class experts to be selling themselves cheaply.

> You expect to pay a large amount of money for an expert.

By the way, there is no fairy waving a magic wand that you have to wait for in order to become the expert in your field. Paul McKenna didn't become the *World's Greatest Hypnotist* because someone told him he was. He assumed that by positioning himself even before he was well-known. Instead of having to climb a ladder to success or positioning, there are a few simple but effective ways to just leap to the top, but it will require you to do some work.

The fastest and most effective way to gain expert status is to write a book. Hang on, hang on! Yes you can. It's really not that hard. I've done it - not just with this one, but my first book, *'101 Naked Confessions of a Gay Hairdresser: Quick, Dirty and Uncensored Secrets to Perfect Hair From the World's Most Outrageous Hairdresser'* was exactly a study in creating an expert. At the time I had made my then business partner - Terry Wilson - the face of the salon. He became the *World's Most Outrageous Hairdresser* by default. He didn't earn the title from a public vote, he just assumed it, and the book scaled the deal.

Writing a book takes time but it's really not that difficult. I've given you three simple ways to do it in *The Appendix.*

## Alpha Positioning

I'm not talking about alpha males or females here. The alpha male or female in social animals is the one with the highest rank. What I'm talking about is more to do with how you portray yourself to your clients, and how much you let your clients dictate to you.

---

## What it really boils down to is: are you going to let others do your thinking for you?

---

Because that's the decision you are making when you procrastinate and let others influence you with their opinion. This includes popular media such as newspapers, TV, magazines and social media, as well as the people around you - even clients.

One great example of the stupidity of taking your opinions from social media is the anti-vaccination groups or so called 'anti-vaxxers'. The majority of these deluded cockwombles have formed their opinions and decisions based on unsubstantiated information that 'do-gooder' (*"I'm just here because of concern for humanity"*) dregs have posted in the various groups. No evidence exists for the claims that are made against vaccines, but people continue to let others do their thinking for them by taking on the rhetoric of the influencers who prey on the weak and gullible. You only have to read a few of the posts on any given group to realise the stupidity and even the sheer ugly nastiness of some of these rejects. And worst of all, they sell 'hope' or the 'illusion of hope' in the form of 'alternative healing'.

It is astounding how many people let themselves be influenced by others. Alpha positioning tips this on its head by saying, *"My business, my rules"*. You are entitled to your opinion but if you want my product or service, your opinion is invalid to the way I run my business.

If you can't take me, my personality or how I run my business, get off my list. But if you want to make a success of yourself then buy my product. In the words of the legendary American author Napoleon Hill (he wrote the bestselling *'Think and Grow Rich'*): *"If you are influenced by the opinions of others you have no desire of your own."*

And the Alpha Queen Bitch agrees.

## Powerful Differentiation

Hairdressing and the beauty industry is a heavily commoditised market. This means that it is a market dominated with undifferentiated products and services, such as shampoo or haircuts, which are characterised by a low profit margin. A lot of people supply haircuts so the choice of hairdressers is huge and clients can buy on price if they choose.

One way to prevent this is to position yourself with a point of difference, and I'm not necessarily talking about a USP (unique selling point/proposition), it's more about putting the one thing that no one else has into your marketing and your business: your personality.

*'101 Naked Confessions of a Gay Hairdresser'* is a perfect example of positioning and differentiating yourself in your market. How many hairdressers have written a book? Not very many, and most of the ones that have are autobiographical and have been penned long after success. Even a search for hairdressing books brings up textbooks for hairdressing students, children's books about how to get your reluctant child to have a haircut, and picture books showing hair trends over time.

But if you could write a book that would appeal to your market and provide valuable information on beauty and haircare, it would definitely make you stand out. I will go more into the process of becoming an author a bit later, but you are not limited to books. You can put your personality into your daily emails, your monthly newsletter, your website, or anything else you can think of.

It can be uncomfortable to start with, but what's a little pain for long-term gain? And consider this: if you are not going to be the face of the salon, pick someone who can be. Selling is about a person, not the thing. When I started marketing my salon in this way, Terry and I agreed that he would be the face of the salon, just because he was in there most of the time. He was also a very colourful personality to have about. Everything I wrote in *'101 Naked Confessions of a Gay Hairdresser'* covered true Terry stories; I just put them into readable format.

*It can be done.*

## Polarisation

Polarisation is the ability to take a position and stick with it, even though it means that not everyone will agree with you, or like you, or want to do business with you. But as I said earlier, you don't care, you don't want to do business with everyone anyway. You want to do business with the right people, the people who are a best fit for you and your business. Not many people have the balls to do this. But if you take a stance and say, *"The big Sky Daddy is a load of bollox,"* you'll attract people who agree with you and like you for your honesty. At the same time, you'll repel those who are opposed.

A more relevant example is to say that you will not accept anyone in the door of the salon who will not use your products. Here's why: you know your products work (I'm assuming here that you have a quality service and products and you know that they work well - no cheap, shitty products that you cut corners with, or 20-minute blowdries that all look the same), and if your clients use your products they are going to see the results and love you. When they love you they are going to want to come back for more.

Lather, rinse, repeat.

Anyone who is not prepared to do this is going to have problems. You're going to end up having to fix them and listen to their complaints, or they are going to go elsewhere anyway.

Don't forget it takes more effort and investment to find a new client than it does to keep one.

Polarising your clients beforehand acts like a filter.
It lets the good ones in and keeps the bad ones
out.

The beauty of Polarisation is that it is not hard. It's closely linked to differentiation and putting your own personality in your business.

I'll say that again, because it's worth repeating: *put your personality in and on your business. People buy from people and your people are buying you.*

And get this: it's fun. It's much less effort than trying to be something you are not. Or trying to be like other competitors. In fact, even the idea of a competitor becomes redundant when you put yourself in your marketing, because your clients are no longer buying the thing, they are buying you.

And only *you* can sell *you*.

## Chapter 4. Summary

→ **Positioning is how you orientate yourself, your image, your behaviour and the message you give out.** Premier Positioning is doing that to the high-end.

→ **Your business, your rules.** Everyone comes into your business by your invitation.

→ **Decide your own worth.**

→ **Become the expert.** Assume the mantle by being the best in your niche.

→ **Stand out in a commoditised market by putting your personality into your business.**

→ **Polarise prospective clients by taking a position and sticking to it.** You will attract clients who like it and agree with it, and repel those who don't.

### Take Action

Decide your niche right now – your expert area. Forget about being a general salon. What will you focus on? Which area are you the most expert in? Take a look at your figures and determine which services give you the highest percentage of clients. That's your niche.

# CHAPTER FIVE

# PREMIUM PRICING – THE EASIEST WAY TO MAKE MONEY

Have you heard the one about the Russian woman who came into the salon and wanted her waist-length, thick, damaged hair changed from dull orange to a healthy creamy blonde, and was prepared to sit in the chair for the day to get it? Putting aside the fact that this may not be your ideal client and her expectations may be too high, how much do you think she was prepared to pay?

The answer is, she didn't even ask what the price would be. She just wanted a solution to her problem – turning her long, damaged, orange hair into long silky creamy blonde hair. And she was prepared to do whatever was required for the convenience. The salon charged double their highest rate, and she didn't bat an eyelid. Then she asked, *"Does anyone know the best plastic surgeon in London?"* as that was where she was off to next. The salon should have charged 10 times the amount…

Very few people buy on price. Don't believe me? Consider this…

If everyone bought on price, every driver would have a cheap car and there would be no luxury vehicles, such as the Maserati. We would all travel by tube, not fast trains, there would be no Hiltons as we would all stay in Travelodges, and there would only be £10 crack whores and no £4000 per night escorts.

---

Premium Pricing is not only possible, it makes for a far more pleasurable business, in more ways than one.

---

When we talk about price a whole lot of emotions come out

based on our beliefs around money. Beliefs handed down to you by your parents and your peers and your interpretation of the world. And because we are talking about emotions, rather than logical thought, those beliefs are almost always wrong. Price does not generally matter to your client.

The reality is, what your clients really want is reliability of the product and service and yourself. They're also looking for convenience, speed, accurate and bespoke solutions to problems, availability, easy relationships, predictability, flexibility, accuracy with deliveries, honesty, openness and clear communications.

Got all that?

Good.

So if that is what they want, and price doesn't come into it, what's the benefit of raising your prices?

Well, at the risk of stating the fucking obvious, you will make more money.

**Let's reverse it:**

Say you have a treatment that you sell for £135 and you make a profit of £35 per treatment, and you then discount the price by 10% in order to 'compete' with 'Bargain Clips' around the corner. Now your treatments are £121.50 and you are only making a £21.50 profit per treatment. That's a decrease in profit of 38.6%.

As an aside here, if you cut your prices and have to sell more treatments to get the same income, could you cope with the volume?

But now let's say you had your original treatment price of £135 and you increased the price by 10%. No one worth dealing with will object to a 10% price increase (and it doesn't have to be 10%, a 1% price increase in some cases could be enough to bring in a significantly larger income, and there's nothing to stop you increasing your prices by 50% or 75% or 500%), now your treatment is £148.50, with a profit of £48.50: an increase overall of 38.6%.

What would a 38.6% increase in profits mean to your business?

Oh, and another thing, inflation is a given. Not increasing your prices is a de facto price cut. Say you don't increase your prices in 10 years, your own costs are rising so you are seriously taking a hit with a massive price cut. Remember, nobody makes you cut your prices except yourself.

> Here's the thing, we only buy something to solve a problem.

What's a problem for you is not a problem for me. And what is a problem now may not be a problem later, and so on.

Take, for example, someone with dry, frizzy hair. There is no way I would buy something that tamed it, as I don't have that problem. But anything to do with keeping my hair blonde instead of green with all the swimming I do is a different story.

What makes a frizz ball head lie awake at night with desire will be the problem they want solved, such as to smooth their frizz and have soft, bouncy hair. A value is purely subjective - value to a frizz ball to tame her hair is not value to me. Value to me would be a spray-in product that protects my hair from chlorine. Yes, both are the same thing, a problem being solved, but they are as far apart as a crack whore's legs on benefits day.

So, if you are providing value – a fine dining experience, a smoothing treatment, an anti-chlorine spray that works - you will attract the right type of client. This client will not just be interested in the price; this client will be interested in having their problem solved. And they tend to be a better class of client because of it. People with more skin in the game, so to speak, are more amenable to your suggestions, are politer and will give you more respect. The whole process becomes more pleasurable for you and your client. And that's what you want out of business, isn't it?

If you are getting price buyers, you haven't given them sufficient reason to see the value in what you are selling. Price then becomes the default comparison between your product or service and the guy's down the road, as that is all they've got.

Your choice as a business owner is about whom you're going to serve. Most of your competitors will take any business they can get — and because there are infinitely more chavs, ragamuffins and guttersnipes than there are affluent and high-quality people out there, catering for the masses means you're going to suck up the dregs whether you intend to or not - unless you take it upon yourself specifically, to cater only to the top-end.

> Price is incredibly elastic, and we are all guilty of underpricing.

I learnt this years ago when I was working as a manager for the corporate arm of a large Antipodean travel company. I had a portfolio of business clients, and essentially my job was to book their travel for them. Now, back in the day, agents who sold travel would get reasonably good (10-12%) commissions from airlines or hotels for selling their flights or rooms, and if you worked at a large travel company you might also have access to negotiated prices that weren't available to the public. These 'net fares' were used to sell the same flight or hotel to a client, but you could choose your own commission to put on top of it.

The trick was to establish a relationship with the clients so that they then depended on you for everything; every change to a flight time, every room upgrade, even, in the case of one arsehole, to make sure that each hotel in any country he visited had an ATM within 10 metres, and a gym with the correct weights in it. Because then I could add some pretty exceptional commissions to the fares and they wouldn't bat an eyelid, have a fit or raise a query. And it wasn't just £50 here or there, the biggest commission I made on one booking was £10,800 for just six flights around Asia. And the only reason I made that commission was that I had put £5000 on the client's previous booking and they didn't squeak.

You may think that this is unethical but a) I don't really give a fuck and b) the client was getting value, he had my personal mobile number so he could ring me any time of the day or night to make instant changes to his bookings, something that was a priority for him.

As I said before, prices are incredibly elastic; there is no such thing as 'the going rate'. Premium prices also infer a higher quality product or service. When you compare a £25 hair cut with a £250 haircut, you are not going to expect much with the former, but you'll want a damn good night out with the latter.

If a client is questioning the price, that means they can't see the value in your proposition, and this gives you the perfect opportunity to keep talking to them and sell on the back of it. And this is what you can say if they do query the price: *"You can have any two of these - top quality, exceptional service, or low price, but you can't have all three."*

> When offered the choice, in the main, people will give up the low price before anything else.

And when your prices are high you are held accountable to the value that the client sees. You will go out of your way to provide a high-end product or service. You will also get better compliance and consumption from your client, which means that they will follow through with your product or service. They will get the value out of it and hopefully, if you are doing it right, come back for more.

Take a £5000 conference versus a free seminar; it's probable that the people attending the conference are more likely to take action and benefit themselves in the process, not only because they have more skin in the game, but also because they will be better qualified to begin with. They are more likely to be implementers or action-takers because they already have the means and the wherewithal to pay for and attend a £5000 event.

Take this example again: a £5000 conference is likely to attract a smaller number of committed clients, but you can spend more time and effort on those clients than filling a room with hundreds of freebie seekers, which will force you to give a higher value service.

Win win.

So, premium pricing can make you a shit-load of money, but when you combine it with premier positioning in the overall strategy, you can watch your profits skyrocket.

The advantages of premium pricing are immense, and given that raising your prices is the easiest thing you can do straight away, the benefits should outweigh your reservations.

**With premium pricing you:**

- **Make more money.** As demonstrated with the example of raising the price of a treatment, your profit doesn't just grow, it grows exponentially. For each % price rise, the profit % grows in multiples.

- **You get a better class of client.** As un-PC as this sounds, peasants are a fact of life, but you don't have to lower yourself to sell to them or pander to their whining. People who buy on price tend to be slow to pay, if at all, and moan and complain about it. Who would you prefer to be doing business with?

- **You work less for it.** What do you think is easiest to sell: a hundred £10 haircuts or one £1000 haircut?

- **It's in the buyer's favour.** People like and trust you, which means you have integrity. You've proved it over the time you have spent with them. You demonstrate value to people, and to them that price is worth paying.

- **You feel better and so do your staff.** Not only is it satisfying to sell at a higher price, but also not dealing with peasants means you don't get dragged down into their icky little world. It creates a nicer environment for your staff to work in, and if they work on commission, their pocket also benefits. Win win.

- **You get better compliance from your clients.** If you ask them to keep their hair maintained after a service, they are more likely to if they have paid a premium price for it, and the same goes for selling premium-priced, high-quality products too. This is really important, as if they don't follow your instructions they won't get the results and they won't come back. That actually means that you are giving them a better value service in the long term. You can also provide a better service and give them more individual attention. You are spending less time with many clients at £10 each, which means you can spend more time with one client at £1000 per time.

## What's more important than price?

- ✓ **Quality and service.** It's a given now that you should be providing exceptional service (and products) to your clients. It's not a USP. People expect that with higher pricing. If you are not already giving exceptional service, then you need to sort that out.

- ✓ **Reliability.** If you buy anything you want it to work. And you want it to work well. In general, cheap implies lower quality, and inevitably you will need to replace it when it doesn't work or it breaks.

- ✓ **Status and recognition.** We all love an ego boost (which is kind-of why luxury brands do so well).

- ✔ **Peace of mind.** We'll all happily pay a premium if we know that this is going to solve our problem. If you have ever been in chronic pain you will know that cheap paracetamol no longer takes the edge off, but a codeine-based drug at double the price, is going to relieve that pain pretty quickly and solve the problem.

- ✔ **Convenience.** If you have everything your client wants, it's more attractive than them having the hassle of going out and sourcing every component themselves.

- ✔ **Speed.** Instant gratification is a big problem in society, but that's the point: we all want it and we'll pay for it. Which is why Amazon Prime does so well.

- ✔ **Done-for-you.** The ultimate in laziness. But this also goes hand in hand with peace of mind and reliability. As much as home-colour boxes sell by the millions, there are also millions of women who will buy the service from a salon for the same reasons.

## How do you know what price to charge?

Test it. There is no right or wrong answer to this, other than right now, you almost certainly are not charging enough. You won't know what your client is prepared to pay until you put the price out there. I suspect you have probably had a look at the other salons around you and pitched yours similar to theirs. The question is: have they got their prices high enough? Where did they get their prices? Probably the same place you did. To paraphrase a famous quote: *"The majority is always wrong."* If the statistic were true - that 80% businesses go out of business within the first five years of trading - why would you want to follow what everybody else is doing? There is only one exception to this, which you can do as an exercise: Look around and see who is the most expensive player in the hair and beauty industry right now and then answer these questions:

1. **What are they doing?**

2. **How are they doing it?**

3. **How can you do it better?** Or, if you can't beat them, what can you take from them and use to create your own high-value niche within the same wider market?

## How To Increase Your Prices

### Price ratcheting

This is one of the simplest ways to make more money fast, and it works better than any other tactic in marketing. Add 10% onto a service, then, in two months time, add another 10%, then another and another, until you either start getting price resistance from your clients or the sales you are making from the drop off of clients (and you will get this) is greater than the net profit you are making from the price increase.

If you are not comfortable with the thought of raising your prices, bear in mind that your business profits are at the mercy of inflation anyway. Unless you cut your business costs every year, you will have a natural rise in costs with inflation, so you will need to raise your prices just to cover the rent at some point, or you're going to go down the gurgler.

### Be bold with a select service

Could you take your highest-selling service and charge it at 10x its amount? Why not? Will you lose clients? Probably. Will you attract a different type of client for whom price is not an issue, providing you are giving good value? Probably. You can only test and see. But I will tell you this, once you let go of your own emotional responses around money and pricing you will not look back.

### Bundle your services and products

Put a service or two together with a product or two, call it something other than what you already call it, give it a little non-monetary value and sell it for a higher price than its component parts.

---

*Real Life Example*

I bundled a series of treatment services, (a take home shampoo, conditioner and treatment, and a bespoke service) for £600. The client had to be 'selected' for eligibility for the treatments, had to pay upfront and had to commit to six weeks of sequential appointments (The first one was two hours and then they had a single, one hour appointment per week). The guarantee was baby-soft hair in six weeks if they followed the regime to the letter, or 100% of their money back. The component parts for the products cost a total of £60, and paying a stylist to do it cost £139, leaving me with a gross profit of £401. The same services, if booked separately with no compliance, would have brought in £235, and that's only if the client rebooked for treatments each time they came in.

---

### Charge for what others are giving away for free

Do you have a 'free consultation' as part of your service? Why not charge a premium price for it instead, with a cast-iron 100% money-back guarantee to overcome resistance over the premium price? You will then attract clients who really want what you are offering and are more committed to making it work than someone just waltzing off the street for a quick wham bam thank you and goodbye.

### Reinvent the method

Take what you are doing and make it into a complete

experience. Think about what Richard Branson did for air travel. Air travel is getting from one point to another in a metal tube in the sky. It can be done by anyone who is prepared to pay for the privilege, but Richard decided that the 'experience' should be the value, and so he came up with a bar you could sit at in the middle of the plane, spa treatments onboard, sleeper suits for overnight flights, etc.

What could you do to your salon to turn it into an 'experience'? It could be 'by invitation only' - no walk ins. Have private rooms with the person's name on the door, decked out with all their favourite things - drinks, music, magazines, personalised gowns... Create a package for overseas guests where you buy them the flight, the hotel, the services at the salon, the VIP list to the club, or tickets to the show for them and a friend?

---

Reinvention is only limited by your imagination and your balls, and you can premium price the shit out of these ideas.

---

## Upsell

Sell the deluxe package, the super deluxe package or the uber deluxe package of whatever service they are getting. If you don't tell them what is available, they don't know. They may just stick with the original package, or they may surprise you.

**Premium Pricing and Premier Positioning work well together and there are a couple of reasons why:**

### Pain of disconnect

If you have cracked the value nut and are attracting loyal, salivating clients to partake in your premium-priced services, they are more likely to stay with you for some time, and, even cooler, they generally won't bat an eyelid if you continue to raise the price of something they are already regularly buying from you. This is known as the *'pain of disconnect'.*

The benefits your clients are receiving from you are greater than what would happen to them if they had to do it themselves, or even look for someone else. For example, my personal trainer charges a fairly high price compared to other trainers I've had, but I'll happily pay it as I get value from his service. Not only am I getting my butt whipped into shape, but also he is helping me with fitness, weight loss and muscle tone so that I can achieve some of the very specific goals I have. Unlike every other trainer I've had, which usually involved one or two workout sessions a week at their gym, Jaydyn comes to me, uses all the facilities I have to mix it up and keep it interesting (the gym, the pool, the beach), gives me a weekly meal plan (punishes me if I don't stick to it), oversees my programme in the flesh twice a week and makes me 'check in' every day to see where I hurt and how I am feeling. He also tailors a DIY programme based on that information for the days when he doesn't see me (and he expects a check in again when I've done it). Because he has given me so much value, he could charge what he liked and I would be prepared to pay it (to a point, I admit). This is because the pain of losing him (because of the benefits the training is giving me) would be too difficult (as are the 100 squats mixed with burpees).

### I'm not for everyone

There's a psychology, which roughly translates as, *"I have what you want but I might not necessarily give it to you, even if you really, really, really want it like a crack addict on payday."*

---

### Real Life Example

A friend of mine lives on the Channel Island of Jersey. She was in the market for a hairdresser and asked the locals who they would recommend. They came up with the name of a French

---

hairdresser. My friend duly went to the salon and asked to make an appointment for a blow dry to test him out. She was told that there was no possible way she could see the stylist as he was booked up six weeks in advance (she said this even though there was no one in the salon), and he was very expensive so she probably couldn't afford him. Well, my friend went away thinking *"how rude"*, but the whole situation niggled her and she became determined to get an appointment with this stylist, at this salon, regardless of cost and regardless of how long she would have to wait. And she would bloody well have a full colour and cut instead of just a blow dry. So she called back and made the appointment for six weeks in advance. Three weeks later there was a 'cancellation' and she instantly accepted the appointment, even though it was not convenient for her. Was the service of value? Yes, even though she paid three times the amount of what was quoted to her at another more accommodating salon. Was the stylist so busy he couldn't see her for six weeks? Probably not, but this example shows how Premier Positioning and Premium Pricing work hand in hand to attract your ideal client and repel the ones who are not.

### What about discounts?

Let's address the elephant in the room: the foul-smelling discount.

Don't ever be confused between your 'offer' when it comes to selling and 'discounts'.

Discounting or price-cutting is always a self-inflicted wound and works in complete opposite of profit growth.

The danger of discounts is that you make less money and you send the wrong message to your market by saying that you are prepared for *them* to make the rules not *you*, and you can get yourself in deep shit. Once you start discounting for clients it's a slow and painful death-spiral, as it is hard to stop.

And yes, in my opinion, I would run a mile from discount coupon operators who advertise your service to their list at a huge reduction. For many reasons this is growth suicide - not least because their lists are filled with price-buying chavs, peasants and commoners who shop from discount voucher to discount voucher and will never be your ideal client, even if you 'wow' them with your service. A *very limited few* will stay with you.

If you are looking for a quick cash flow fix, there are much better ways that won't compromise your positioning or prevent you from attracting the right type of buyer.

If you must discount, a much better way is the BOGOF offer - Buy One Get One Free - where, if priced right, you make the same profit as selling one, and you get a better class of client.

## Chapter 5. Summary

→ **Very few people buy on price.**

→ **If you are getting price buyers, you are not showing enough value for your products and services.**

→ **People only buy because they want to solve a problem.**

→ **Price is elastic and you are almost certainly not charging enough right now.**

→ **Raising your prices is the easiest way to make more money *immediately*.**

→ **Clients want more than a low price.** They want reliability, status and recognition, peace of mind, convenience, speed, and a done-for-you service.

→ **There are a number of ways to increase your prices without losing customers:** price ratcheting, being bold with a select service, bundling, selling what others give away for free, reinventing the method and upselling.

→ **Beware of the foul-smelling discount**: it's a downward spiral to doom.

*Take Action*

Raise your prices today. Go on. ***Do it.***

## CHAPTER SIX

# THE SUBTLETIES OF SELLING – THE ART OF SEDUCTION

I want to talk about the important distinction between Transactional and Transformation Selling, which will throw a curve-ball across what you have been trained to know selling to be. And more importantly, the selling/buying experience for your client.

Selling, when done seductively, is a graceful performance of entertainment and flow, one that is mutually enjoyable to all parties involved. There are some very simple rules involved in selling, but the complexity around the way these rules interplay is fascinating, and I am sure you will find plenty of material on the art of selling in bookshops and the net. But I want to focus on two types of selling here: *Transformational* and *Transactional* Selling. Transformational Selling is the graceful, seductive process and Transactional Selling is as clumsy and shocking as a physical assault. At best Transactional Selling leaves you ambivalent, at worst it leaves you battered and weary.

Nido Qubein is the man behind the terminology here.

Have you heard of him?

No?

Nido is a self-made businessman who arrived in the US in 1966 as a teenager with $50 in his pocket. He now has a net worth of $75-100 million. I think he knows his stuff. So let's take a deeper look into what these two types of selling are.

## Transactional Selling

My daughter is learning how to sail and spends a couple of hours on the water each week. As we live somewhere quite warm (understatement), keeping hydrated is a big priority, and we don't go anywhere without drinking water. When she is out in her little yacht she needs to take in fluids and we've gone through many different options for water containers.

I don't like buying little bottles of water for one-off use because of the plastic consumption, so that's a no. She's had reusable plastic water bottles but the water gets warm in them and she doesn't like to drink it. I've bought expensive, insulated thermos bottles which she has managed to leave behind, or damage, or get stolen. And I am always concerned that anything going in the boat will end up at the bottom of the sea when she capsizes.

So doing the research, and with the backing of a recommendation from another mum, I bought her a Camelbak backpack. Now this is a great invention as it is basically a bladder that fits into a small, light backpack, and has a long hose coming out of the bladder which you pull over your shoulder. At the end of the hose is a valve and a rubber 'bite'. You put the rubber bite in your mouth and whenever you need water you bite down and water is released.

So far, so genius.

There is a slight flaw in the design though, in that if you get too aggressive with your bite, or just through general wear and tear over the passage of time, the rubbery bite can get holes in it through which the water from the bladder leaks uncontrollably. Like in the sailing bag, or in the car. Camelbak are prepared for this though and sell the valves and the bites independently.

So, as my daughter had been getting a bit chompy with her bite, I was in the market for a new one. I walked into a big sports store looking for such a thing, and doing what I do best to get things done more efficiently, I asked a sales assistant where I could find one. He led me to the Camelbak stand (which I had walked past), picked a packet off the shelf, handed it to me and said, *"This is what you need, a Big Bite".* Then he led me to the cashier, I paid and left.

This is Transactional Selling. A client walks into your store, they browse, buy something they want and then leave.

Transactional Selling takes the buyer from the unknown to the known.

You don't know or care what their problem is, you just have the product they may want.

**Transactional Selling has the following characteristics:**

1. **It's a one-off hit, and relies on the chance that the client will see the 'thing' on a sales page, or be in your store and in the mode to purchase straight away.**

2. **It's a numbers game.** It relies on many new clients over and over again making a purchase.

3. **There is no follow up with the client.** It's a wham, bam, and thank you ma'am scenario. Quick, dirty, doesn't call back.

4. **There is no relationship with the client after the initial interaction.** In fact, the initial interaction is almost as devoid from the relationship as the follow up. Nada. Not interested, just take my 'widget' or service because that's all I have and that's what you need.

5. **One-size fits all.** The solution offered to the client is only one option. It's like a toothbrush salesman saying that his toothbrush is all you need because you have teeth. There is no bespoke product or service based on your actual needs and desires.

6. **There is no personality involved in the sale.** You'll be lucky to get a name of the salesperson if they are wearing a badge.

7. **As there is no differentiation between the service and**

**product based on the characteristics above, there is no added value to you so you will probably shop on price.** And the sales person will be limited to selling on price and compete on price.

8. **The transaction is therefore driven by the client.**

9. **There is no plan or strategy to selling more to the client after the initial sale.**

10. **The type of client you attract with this type of selling is not one you want in your business – price buying, whingers and moaners.**

## Transformational Selling

Compare that with *Transformational Selling* and let's go back to the store where I bought my big rubber bite.

How differently could the salesperson have acted when he had a captured prospect in his store? Well, for a start he could have asked me what the Camelbak was used for and he would have got a pretty good answer about my daughter and sailing. Which is a start to mining the seam of gold my daughter's activities opens up, i.e., my wallet.

Then he should have shown me some options and helped me make a decision based on the best product for my needs and desires. Then he could have chatted about sailing, or children, to try and upsell me on any of those related topics (vast and bottomless from my experience).

Then he should have taken my details and started emailing me or contacting me regularly to build a relationship with a view to selling me more of the same: *"It might be time to replace your Big Bite"*; more of something related: *"Are your sailing shoes becoming a bit tight with growing feet? We have the answer..."*; or sell something different: *"We know you like to play outdoors, check out this new bike, built specifically for riding in the giant sandpit."*

What he should not have done was let me leave the building without at least trying to protect his asset, i.e., me, from being poached by the next store selling something similar. Because that's what Transformational Selling is all about.

> Transformational Selling is establishing a relationship with a prospect, taking them from the known to the unknown – I know you have a problem but I also know that you have more than just that problem and I have solutions custom-made for you personally.

Find out where they are and then where you can take them with your bespoke service. There are no guarantees that you can solve their whole problem, but you will have a number of options for them that will get results.

**There are many reasons why salon owners don't take this approach with every prospect, but I will give you two:**

1.  **It takes time.** Selling something once is dead simple, provided you have the means to get a constant stream of new clients through the door to sell to once. Realising that the profit is in the lifetime value of the client means that the relationship with the client is the most important thing, not the one-off sale. And all good relationships take time.

2.  **It means work.** Oh shit. If you are unfit and unhealthy you don't take action until the pain of being unfit and unhealthy outweighs the pain of doing something about it, i.e., changing your diet and exercising. Most salon owners are like that – not necessarily unfit and unhealthy, but not feeling the pain enough to change. It will take the pain of doing marketing to be less than the pain of constantly losing money, or worrying about cash flow, or how to pay the wages, to actually get on and do the work.

Most will do nothing, which is where you have an advantage just by following the information in this book. But I digress.

**Here are the lessons we can learn from this:**

**Lesson No.1:** Nothing changes until it hurts too much to leave it the way it is. Not only does this apply to your own business, but it applies to your clients and prospects too.

**Lesson No.2:** Things get easier with practice and experience. This applies to everything, from exercising to marketing, and everything in between.

**Lesson No.3:** Sometimes it takes a short (or even a long) while to start seeing the results, even though you know what you're doing is working. You can see this with any weight loss regime.

*Significant results take time.*

It's just the same with Transformational Selling, which involves thinking about your business, and running it, very differently. And as I have already said, salon owners tend not to do this due to the mere thought of the pain of doing it.

Transformational Selling involves getting someone on board and keeping them there. (Not in an unethical way by the way.)

**Transformational Selling has the following characteristics:**

1. **It looks at lead generation, not the single sell off the page.** You don't even look to buy a client; you look to acquire a relationship with someone in order to sell to them further down the line.

2. **There is a structured approach to sales and upsells, and a focus on processes and systems.**

3. **The client receives bespoke, detailed solutions rather than a 'one-size-fits-all' approach.** You may use the same strategies but the outcome will be different for each client. Everyone gets a bespoke, tailored experience.

4. **The focus is on the lifetime client value of a person.** The higher proportion of my profit is in my long-term relationship with you, and it's the same with your clients. The longer they are with you the more money you make from them, but also their cost to you goes down. It's long-term thinking.

This results in the business being driven by the business owner, for the business owner. You are in control of your business.

And that's where you want to be, right?

*Right.*

## Chapter 6. Summary

→ **Transactional Selling is a clumsy, brutal, one-off sale.** It benefits neither the buyer nor the seller in the long-term.

→ **Transformational Selling is a slow seduction, which enables you to build a relationship with a client, with an aim to continue to sell to them over their lifetime.**

→ **The bulk of your profits are with Transformational Selling.**

### Take Action

I am going to give you a break in this chapter, but you are going to have to do some research. Have a look at your selling process. Do you have one?

# CHAPTER SEVEN

# RELATIONSHIPS – SACK YOUR CLIENTS

If you implement the chapter on positioning, in particular the part about polarisation and repelling the clients who are not going to be the best fit for you, then you won't have the problem I'm going to mention. But if you haven't and you have challenging clients who are making your life and your business miserable, here's what you can do: sack the bad ones. You know the expression, *"One bad apple can rot the whole barrel?"* Well, it's true of your clients too. You don't need my permission, but I'm going to give it to you anyway.

If you were too afraid to do it before, suck it up and do it now:

Sack your bad clients.

Now, if you have done what I have advised in the first instance about determining your ideal client, you should have weeded out the unsuitable ones before they even set foot in the door. For example, if your ideal client is one that listens to what you tell them about their hair or skin routine, and does what you tell them with the products you know will work, then those who are determined to use a cheap product that strips oils or colour would have naturally failed to be selected during the start of your relationship process.

In my line of work, I only deal with business owners who have brains, have been in business for at least three years and have a positive cash flow. But there are times when the odd bad apple will slip through the net.

For example, in my previous business, the policy was that no client was to leave the salon without their hair being finished, i.e., they had to have a blow dry or sit under the climazone until their hair was dry if they wanted their natural curls to shine. We had a number of clients who would insist that they wanted to walk out wet and not pay for that part of the service. Well, little did they know that the service was an all-inclusive price, which wasn't made up of segments. So the price would be the same either way. But, there was also no way we were going to let any client of ours walk out of the salon resembling a drowned rat, as their hair was our advertising, and that is just bad press.

In this kind of situation, you have permission to sack your client. How? By politely indicating that unless they are going to conform to the way you work, and the way you run your business, they would be more comfortable somewhere else. And at this point you can do a double whammy by recommending a competitor. This means that you a) get rid of the problem and b) give a competitor a problem.

I've done this on a number of occasions. One that sticks out in my mind was a client from early on whom I wrote an email about to my list (pay attention, there's a dual lesson here about how to sack clients and how to write emails that sell).

## Real Life Example

Once upon a time, a long time ago, there was a particular client in the salon, let's call her Madam, as that's what she was.

A proper one.

Now madam had regular appointments with us early in the mornings, every Tuesday. This particular Tuesday I am talking about was like any other. Only one small thing was different. Workmen were digging up the road/footpath outside the salon.

Anyway, Madam was having colour put on her hair and the time came when it needed to be washed off before it overdeveloped and left in its wake a nasty shade of nuclear orange. We got her to the basin at the exact moment when the water to the salon was turned off.

Not a trickle.

Not a drip.

Not a vapour.

You guessed it; the workmen had cut us off. They had gone through a pipe, or hit the wrong button, or whatever excuse they usually have for leaving you high and dry without telling you.

So it was panic stations. While I was out there having words with the workmen and saying, *"can't you see that we are a salon and we need water?"* I was also thinking, *"How are we going to deal with this?"* At this point Madam started to kick off at the basin, screeching about her hair. I reassured her that I would get water from the shop next door and that everything would be fine.

I wish I could say that Madam demanded Evian (which would have made a better story), but she didn't. Evian was actually the only water the guy had left in the shop.

So Madam got Evian.

Now, this was the time, early on in the salon days, when I was 'helping out' and learning about everything from the ground up – a bit like McDonalds. To be honest, I was a bit put out at having to learn how to shampoo hair (it is an art form in itself, you certainly know when you get a bad one), as my motto is – not born to serve. But there I was, heating the bottle of water in the kettle to just the right temperature so that it could be poured over Madam's head.

Five bottles later and her hair was clean and shiny.

And in the process she had received personalised attention from two staff, plus a lovely blow dry. Do you think she was grateful at the lengths we went to?

Not a jot.

She complained the whole time about how unprofessional

it was not to have running water in the salon. Complained about the fact that we had used Evian on her hair??!! Actually, she was just one big complaint. You know those people who have nothing nice or positive to say about anything? One of those.

So we sacked her.

Yep, we told her, very nicely, that we were probably not the right salon for her any more as we clearly could not meet any of her expectations. She was a bit shocked at first. I don't think she had been sacked by anyone before. But she eventually got it and we never saw her again.

This is a good thing, trust me. Life is too short to be dealing with that kind of misery all of the time.

## Four Reasons To Sack Your Clients

**Levity aside, this is more important than you think for a number of different reasons:**

1. **If there are whingers, complainers and moaners affecting the mood of the other clients then the vibe of your business suffers.** Have a look at what clients write in testimonials about the ambience of a salon. They are not likely to sit for a two hour treatment where the tension is high.

2. **The confidence of your staff takes a battering if they are having to deal with clients who make their lives a misery.** If this is left it can manifest itself in sick days and poor work practices.

3. **It's just nicer to deal with nice clients who do what you want.** If the products they use are what you have

recommended and they are working, it will be a dream to work with them. It means that you are not having to do the hard repair work; it's just maintenance and getting creative.

4.  **Nice clients will not quibble about price and will actually be your best clients.** They will trust you to deliver and will be your biggest payers.

Once you have sorted out the wheat from the chaff, you are going to want to keep the wheat happy and coming back time and time again. That way you can make bread.

Sorry.

You have worked hard to get them into the salon and their lifetime worth to you is where you will make money. Current clients are five times easier to sell to and spend at least twice as much as a new one. Other than the exceptional products and services you are providing, which are a given, you want to be putting a ring around them and protecting them from wandering off to the next big shiny thing. And if you don't look after them and make them feel like part of the family then they will. If you think of the sports teams or social groups you belong to, you will have a feeling of belonging, being part of a team.

This is what you want to create in your clientele; make them feel that they are part of the group. You want them to feel so good about you, and loyal to you, that they will psychologically feel the pain of disconnect when something else comes into their periphery. You can do this by making sure that you are at the front of their mind whenever they think of their hair or beauty needs.

Fortunately, this is not hard to do; even the smallest thing can create a feeling of belonging. The next chapter, *Relentless Follow up* shares a list of things that you should be doing at the very least, and I will go into further detail about specific ones later in this book. But these are guaranteed to get your clients feeling closer and more loved up!

## Chapter 7. Summary

→ **Again, it's your business, your rules.** If you have clients that don't conform to the way you do business, sack them.

→ **Bad clients affect the whole salon – staff and other clients.** A bad atmosphere can kill a business.

→ **It's far more pleasurable to deal with nice clients than those who piss and moan about everything, including price.**

→ **Your best clients will trust you and are your biggest payers, no quibble.**

### Take Action

This one requires some balls, but I am sure you can do it. Sack your worst clients. Tell them nicely that you are not the best salon for their needs, and they would benefit more from going somewhere else. Recommend a 'competitor'. You get rid of a problem and your 'competitor' gains one.

# CHAPTER EIGHT

## RELENTLESS FOLLOW UP – BUY, DIE OR FLY

**W**hy don't salons follow up leads or walk-in clients?

This happens in every business across the globe, and is one stupid way to leave money on the table, or give away money to other salons down the road. It's ridiculous. Don't believe me? My buddy Vegard, who lives in Norway, sent me a random email with his experience at a salon, and it pretty much sums up what happens:

*Talking about hairdressers...*

*Are most of them fucking morons?*

*I went to get a haircut the other day. Had to try someone new because my 'old' alcoholic barber has had his share of personal issues lately.*

*Anyway, it was actually the owner who cut my hair that day (I don't think she usually does - she has people working for her).*

*We started chatting about business.*

*And what has puzzled me about hairdressers and barbers for a while is why they don't try to book people in to cut their hair more often.*

*Like, I probably should cut my hair every 6 weeks or so. But I always forget and delay because I simply can't be bothered to pick up the phone to schedule an appointment.*

*I asked her if she had a follow up system...Which she didn't.*

*No surprise there.*

*But it didn't seem that she even wanted one. She just sort of shook my questions off and talked about something else.*

*My previous barber was like that too - I asked him several times why he didn't just make new appointments right then and there, and remind customers by text message a day or two before the appointment.*

*His answer was like, "I don't do that kind of thing. I don't want to. I want them to call me when they want their hair cut. I don't want to be pushy."*

*I think a men's cut is like £30 ish.*

*If I should cut my hair every 6 weeks, that's an average of 8 haircuts a year. But I don't. It's probably more like 4 times a year.*

*Say he had 100 customers. If he started following people up, perhaps he could get 30% of his customers to cut their hair every 6 weeks.*

*That's an extra £3600 a year just by sending a few text messages.*

*And stuff like that is dead easy to automate.*

*I just don't get it. It's so bloody simple! AND easy!*

*And they don't even ask me if I want to buy hair gel. If they did I probably would buy. But they don't ask, so I don't.*

*I get that they don't know about - or think about - the possibilities out there.*

*What I can't understand, is why they appear to not WANT to grow their businesses.*

But let's leave Vegard and his rant, and anything to do with your salon business aside for a moment. Let's remind ourselves about the salesperson selling me the Big Bite for my daughter's Camelbak water pack. Where he fell down was that he didn't even attempt to build a relationship with me, find out my problem, tailor a solution, or do any up-selling or cross-selling at all. What he should have done is made sure that he had my details so that he could sell to me again. And again, and again.

Relentlessly.

And you should do the same with your clients.

Until they buy, die, or they ask you to stop.

Most businesses will get the first sale and then do nothing further. Some businesses will make some attempt at following up with the client, but they will usually stop after a couple of contacts.

**Actually, the statistics say:**

→   48% of sales people follow up once with a prospect.

→   25% of sales people make a second contact and stop.

→   12% of sales people only make three contacts and stop.

And yes, you are 'sales people'. The thing is, your client is not always in a space to buy at any particular point in time. They may not need or want your service the day that you decide to send out a text message offer or email them a voucher. It requires relentless follow up from yourself so that you are 'front-of-mind' when the client is in a position to want or need your service.

**And I'll throw some more stats at you:**

→   2% of your sales are made on the first contact with the client.

→   3% of sales are made on the second contact.

→   5% of sales are made on the third contact.

→   10% of sales are made on the fourth contact.

→   80% of sales are made on the fifth to twelfth contact.

So if you are like almost half of all businesses and make no more than one follow up with your prospect you are leaving 98% of your potential income on the table for someone else to come along and pick up.

Utter madness.

## The Hidden Profits Of Relentless Follow Up

Following up relentlessly works because it starts that transformational relationship you are looking for. A relationship that is more profitable, less stressful and more satisfying. The type of relationship where you have fantastic clients you want to work with and are paying you top dollar for the privilege.

**Relentless follow up works because it gives you:**

- ✓ **Almost unlimited bites of the cherry.** A client is only ready to buy when they are ready to buy, and you are there when they are.

- ✓ **Long-lasting profitable relationships.** The more you get to know your client, the more you know what their needs and wants are, and the more you can tailor your products and services to them so that 'selling' becomes easy and pleasurable - for both parties. A long-term loyal client is one who is likely to buy all of your products and services. They may have come in for a basic blow dry, but they will be the ones that also buy your £600 treatment further down the track.

- ✓ **Trust and Authority.** The more your client gets to know you, the more trust they have in you and you will stand out as an authority.

- ✓ **A structured method of sales and up-sells.** Instead of thinking, *"Oh shit, I forgot to sell her some shampoo,"* as she walks out of the door, there is a structured, methodical way of handling each and every client, with no one left behind. Everyone is exposed to the opportunity to buy from you.

- ✓ **Processes, not one-off sales events.** I will talk more about processes a bit further along in this chapter, as it is one of the best ways to get compliance from your staff. To 'do marketing' exactly as you want them to do it. And every time a client is in front of them.

- ✓ **Much bigger lifetime client value.** This is pretty self-explanatory, but if you are relentlessly following up with a client and they are buying more from you, they are worth more to your business.

- ✓ **Great clients.** We buy from people we like; we like people who are like us. Once you've repelled the chavs, peasants and commoners through relentlessly being in their face, the ones who are left will be the ones you like.

- ✓ **A long-term business view and plan.** Instead of jumping from month to month or high-season rush to quiet-time-of-the-year doldrums, you can plan your marketing and make the peaks and troughs redundant.

So, how do you follow up when you have a client who comes in once every two months and you know there is potential to sell something to them in between visits, or increase their number of visits throughout the year?

Well, there are shitloads of ways and some are better than others. You may find you have a favourite method and I've listed a few below. Consider a combination of many of them. That way, no one slips through your net and you eliminate any competition because your clients ain't going anywhere else.

## Eight relentless ways to get in front of your client

1. **Continuity.** Getting your client into a recurring paid membership. This is very simple to do and means you have a guaranteed and known cash flow every month. You can package up your offer so it looks extra valuable to the client.

   They are getting the headache-free ability to have you book all their appointments for them for a year, manage them and feel that they are your priority. You can tier the membership for different levels of price and product too. I'll say more about this in the next section because this is one of the life-changers in your business strategy.

2. **Newsletter.** Free subscription. 4 sides, 1/3 something interesting about yourself, 1/4 about your product or service and the rest about nothing in particular, just something that might interest your clients. For example, a quiz (which you can offer a prize for and ask clients to complete and send back, which makes it interactive).

Post this out to their physical address every month. Ask them to subscribe so they'll only get it if they want it, but then you'll have their postal address, which you can use for other direct mail pieces.

# Hair Organics Herald

Volume 1 Issue 01                                                     January 2014

### Finding a good hairdresser can lead to a lifetime relationship

Terry and I are co-owners of Hair Organics Notting Hill, Terry's the queen, and I'm the 'queen of everything'. Terry and I go way back, you see. I knew Terry back when he was straight. We first met 19 years ago in a small town in the heart of wine country, New Zealand called Blenheim. I had moved there for work and was delighted to find a hairdresser as great as Terry. I loved how I could totally trust him to make me look great. I gave him free reign and I always got compliments on my hair. Knowing I could rely on having great hair made life so much easier. One winter Terry announced he was taking a 6 week holiday in London. He returned from that trip and dropped a bombshell. He had fallen in love with the city and was moving to London for good. I was devastated. Left bereft, I went through the

stress and hassle of finding another hairdresser who was a good match for me. It almost felt like I was reluctantly getting back into the dating world or something. I'm sure you know the feeling - we've all been there. Meanwhile, Terry headed to the UK and we lost touch. Fast forward a few years and my husband and I ended up moving to London for work. Another upheaval. Another search for a new hairdresser. One who got my style. One I got along with. One I could trust to give me hair that is a source of strength and confidence in the midst of my ever-busy life. I once heard a story about two Irish brothers in the 1890s who fled their homeland in search of a better life in America. After getting separated they both unknowingly ended up in New York. Years later they met in a chance encounter on the Brooklyn Bridge, or so the story goes. I was never sure if that tale was true, but I know for sure that this one is...
... One Tuesday evening, shortly after we arrived in London, I was walking down the street in Soho. My eyes were meandering across the storefronts as I passed them by and all of a sudden I caught a glimpse of something. I stopped and looked again. I couldn't believe it. I was standing outside an organic hair salon and there was Terry staring out at me. The rest, as they say, is history.

Kat xxx

*Terry and Kat's cheesiest smiles*

**Eating Your Way to Healthy Hair**

The condition of your hair can tell you a lot about the condition of your health. Over the next few months I am going to share with you how to acheive optimal condition of your hair, starting with the basics that people overlook: Your diet.
Depending on how fast your hair grows, starting a hair-healthy diet today can improve the condition in as little as six months. Add more of these six nutrient-rich foods to your diet and tell me when you start to notice the results.

**Chickpeas**

In addition to providing zinc and folate (nutrients that promote hair health), chickpeas are a great vegetarian source of iron-rich protein, an important combination for hair growth and repair. Be-

**In this Issue:**

*Figure 1. Front page of the Jan 2014 4-page Edition of the 'Hair Organics Herald'*

3.  **Daily emails**. Every day, into their inbox. This is a *Whole Big Subject* in itself, which I will go into in more detail further on, but the main thing is that you will be front-of-mind when they think of hair, which means you'll make money from them.

4.  **Loyalty points**. Most computerised reservation systems have points for money spent in the salon that can be redeemed at future dates.

5.  **Rewards**. A special gift for your top clients, personalised and branded. If not, reward cards work well too. You know the ones I mean - like a coffee card, 'buy five and the sixth one is free' and stamped at the time of service. This works particularly well for things like men's cuts as these can be overlooked in a salon but are often the bread and butter of your bottom line. If you don't want to give away high-end services, have a 'blow dry reward card', for when a client just comes in for a blow dry without colours, etc.

6.  **Telephone calls**. Almost no one does these. I am not talking about a call to remind a client of an upcoming appointment, but an actual telephone call (not text) to a client the week after they have been in for a service. (This works well for both new and existing clients. For the newbies it helps to cement the relationship, for the regulars it's a wow factor that can't be beat as it is so rare.)

    You ask them how they are and how they are enjoying their hair. Then say nothing else, just listen. You will get a variety of responses from delight that you have called, a rave about their hair/colour/style/condition, to a thank you for calling but everything's fine. They may book another appointment or even say, *"It's not quite right,"* and, *"I'm not really sure about it,"* which gives you the opportunity to provide a solution, a fix and get them back in the door.

    I cannot tell you how many times even a little niggle has prevented a new client from returning. Clients very rarely complain and vote with their feet… often you never know why. This phone call is your 'get out of jail free' card.

7.  **Reward your top clients.** Every business will have its top spending clients. Given the 80/20 Principle, it will be the top 20% of your clients that provide you with 80% of your profit. Treat these clients with kid gloves. They are your golden eggs. If you have a points scheme, give these people double or triple. Whatever they want, you give. Whatever you have to give, provide it to these people, and more.

8.  **Service.** It goes without saying that if your service is crap you don't have a business. Or not for very long. It is not enough to say that you provide excellent service. That is the expectation. You need to provide exceptional service, consistently, and this is not your selling point. Service is a given. You should always be looking at creating the most exceptional service and product that ever existed. No shortcuts.

It is better to bring people up to a higher level than to go down to an inferior product. (If you need any more convincing on this, go and read the brilliant book, '*Atlas Shrugged*' by Ayn Rand, it will change how you look at the industry. Especially on the theme of creating a world where everyone charges the same for a service and no one is allowed to aspire to be the best in their field. Ayn Rand wrote the book in 1957, but the same issues she wrote of then apply today. Her philosophy of 'objectivism champions competition', 'creativity' and 'human greatness' is a philosophy I run close to. Be warned though, it will make you angry at the same time.)

The thing most salon owners find difficult is getting staff to consistently give exceptional service in line with the salon's philosophies. This is where 'processes' will be your young, fit, lover.

## *Advanced Bonus: The Skinny On Processes*

Everything you do, whether selling a bottle of shampoo or completing a full head of highlights, can be broken down into a step-by-step process... a process that has actions and an end result that can be measured. This holds true even in a creative industry such as hairdressing, where you want to avoid curbing the creative ambitions of the stylists while offering a consistent service to the client each time.

For example, I broke down our highlighting process into seven simple steps that I expected each stylist to follow. What I was looking for was an end result for the client that was expensive looking, giving fine, natural highlights that looked like they were growing out of the client's head: the holy grail for hairdressing. No 'blonde' wants dark roots where you can tell they are not blonde. Blonde that 'grows out of your head' is the elusive treasure chest. I wasn't looking at placement, colour or tone. I was looking for a process that could be followed by a junior or a new staff member to the letter, enabling them to produce the same result every time, for every client.

This created a high standard in the staff and trust for the clients that someone else could do the job if their regular stylist was away. You have control over quality if you are not there, the client is happy and you are guaranteed the results you want. In turn, you can then improve the process if you need to get optimal performance.

Have general rules in place concerning the process of a client's journey through the salon from lead to follow up. You can do this from opening the salon in the morning through to the micro management of how to secure the salon at the end of the day.

If you have processes, you set expectations that are clear and in writing. This helps prevent miscommunication with staff and interpretations of the rules regarding what is and isn't permissible.

Staff do not always understand (or forget) that owning and running a business is your risk, not theirs. They can always find another job if things go pear-shaped, and are not likely to be around to help you pick up the pieces if you fail. But if they are following your processes you can mitigate that risk and it prevents arguments because it's in writing that can be constantly referred to.

> Everything in your business is a process that can be broken down into simple steps that everyone can follow.

The fewer the steps, the easier they are to learn and get right. When everyone follows the processes you will have consistency through the business, and clients and staff will know what to expect. These processes should be written down and drilled into your staff on all possible occasions. The beauty of this is that if a process is not working you can revisit the steps and find out why.

The step-by-step process stops misunderstandings, miscommunication and creative divas that insist on doing things their way. It also gives you an edge when it comes to selling your business at a later date. If a buyer can step into your business and run it from day one, it's a lot more valuable to you.

So, how does this relate to getting repeat business from your client? Well, imagine that you've done a fabulous job on Mrs Jones and she was all smiles and thank yous as she walked out of the door. But if you do nothing else, your chances of her repeat custom are just that. A chance that is not in your control.

What follows is a step-by-step process that helps put you in control of getting Mrs Jones back in the door. And you can do this until they buy, die, or ask you to go away.

At checkout, Mrs J pays the bill and she is asked if she would like to rebook for her next visit. She says *"Yes,"* and you give her a confirmation and a goody bag, which I will come to, and off she goes. Win. Or she says *"No, not yet,"* or the equivalent, so you give her a goody bag which contains:

- ✔ A referral card giving her a gift and a friend a gift when she refers that friend to the salon. The receptionist explains in detail the benefits and how to use it.
- ✔ A voucher for a free blow dry or an education session: a free session in the salon with her own tools and products on how to use them to create three easy styles at home.
- ✔ Some samples.
- ✔ Some information about the products and the salon's services.

The next day, she receives a thank you email with a voucher for a VIP treatment when she rebooks her next visit. She is now on the daily email list so receives an email every day from the salon owner. A week later she receives a phone call from her stylist just asking how her hair is, and if she is liking it.

Four weeks after the original visit she receives a personalised hand-written card in the mail just saying thank you for being a customer. And she is still receiving daily emails.

There are over half-a-dozen different tactics I have outlined in this process, and it's a great example of a relentless follow up system.

And it is one that works, to great success.

## Chapter 8. Summary

→ **Follow up your clients and potential clients relentlessly until they buy, die, or ask you to stop.**

→ **You are almost certainly leaving money on the table for others to take from you if you don't follow up.**

→ **Relentless follow up allows you long-lasting, profitable relationships, so that you can establish trust and authority.** It is a structured method of sales and upsells, not a one-off sales event. It will give you a much bigger lifetime client value, and increase your profits.

→ **There are a number of ways to follow up:** Continuity membership, newsletters, daily emails, loyalty and reward schemes, phone calls.

→ **Everything in your business can be broken down into simple steps that everyone can follow.** Processes will give your business consistency.

## Take Action

Start writing up your processes. Just do one per day. Start from the opening up of the salon in the morning, and go right through to the closing of it at night.

*Part Two*

# THE
# MEDIUM

# CHAPTER NINE

# ONLINE ADVERTISING – HANGING OFF THE WORLD WIDE WEB

Tactics are the tools or medium you use to get your message to your prospective clients. The thing about tactics is that even though some have been around for a very long time, such as newspaper advertising or direct mail, the landscape changes as technology advances and new tactic platforms are launched (Facebook or LinkedIn advertising), or they alter (Google's algorithms for SEO), or they disappear even (Myspace).

It's wrong to think that any one tactic is the be-all and end-all of getting a continuous stream of clients through your door. But that's what a lot of the shit-peddlers in the marketing industry will try to sell you.

On their own, tactics are nothing.

You can advertise all you like in a glossy magazine, but if your overall strategy is not in place, there will be nowhere for your leads to go and you will be left relying on a transactional sell, something you cannot control, as it is at the whim of the lead.

If you hear someone say: *"YouTube advertising is the next big thing for making you loads of cash,"* be very sceptical, then run a mile. YouTube advertising can be very effective for many industries, and may even work very well for you, but if your strategy is not in place you can kiss bye-bye to a lot of money very quickly, with little or no return on investment.

Another note about tactics is that some are more effective than others, depending which industry you are in. At the time of writing this, it seems that LinkedIn advertising is more effective if you are selling your products or services to other businesses

(B2B), and Facebook advertising is more effective if you are selling products or services directly to individuals as clients (B2C). But that may not always be the case, so you have to test. Again, if 'everybody is doing it,' the time has come to do something different - the majority is always wrong.

Tactics work because they are the principles of marketing to people that have been tested and proven over time. They will continue to work as long as humans remain hardwired as they are now, which means they will continue to rely on psychology and the structure and behaviour of groups of people and markets.

In short, tactics are the short-term implementation of your long-term strategy.

So let's take a look at some of them.

## Online Advertising

What is it?

Online advertising is anything you create digitally and hang off the big, bad World Wide Web. Simple. The internet is vast, it holds massive amounts of data, it's easy and convenient and, provided you have a good internet service provider (ISP), is pretty reliable.

There are a large number (growing by the day) of platforms that you can advertise on to get your message in front of your ideal client/lead/prospect. Just don't forget to pick the ones where your prospect is more likely to hang out. And play strictly by the rules the platform sets. It belongs to them after all (which is why you should not rely on just one - it is beyond your control how they run and if they will still be around in a day, a month or a year from now).

Play strictly by the rules that your country sets for internet use too - you've been warned...

In this section I will look at your website and the main online advertising platforms, but there are lots of others: the choice is up to you.

## Website and landing pages

Is your website a shrine to your creative abilities, with funky pictures, moving sliders, bright colours, squiggly font, and the most ridiculous five words ever written on it (more on those later)? Don't worry, you are not alone, but after you have read this chapter and implemented the changes I am about to recommend, you will have a site that is functional, has a purpose and gets back into its box of what it is designed to do: be a small but working part of your overall strategy.

Yes, your business should have a website, but no, you don't have to have a 10-page, all-singing, all-dancing confection of how amazing you are.

> The most important thing on your website is your visitor.

It's not to show how good your 'branding' is, or how flash your salon looks, or how avant-garde your hairstyles are, and it certainly isn't a photo album with a rotating gallery. Only you and your mother care about your 'images', and even she is probably pretending. Your website is not all about you. Your website is all about your prospect's problem and it tells them how you can provide the solution to it in exchange for their details.

Oh, and the most ridiculous five words on your website are... *"Hi, welcome to our website."* But I will go into that more when it comes to content.

Websites should exist solely to get lead captures, i.e., for your prospective client or lead to opt-in to your email sequence or a free report so that you have their details and can start a relationship with them. This way you can establish trust and get them into your salon when they are comfortable with making that decision.

It doesn't have to be a free report or email sequence either, although these work particularly well and are easy to do. You could have a landing page (a page not published on your website for general view, that your prospect 'lands' on when you advertise it) where you give away:

- A book
- A CD or DVD
- Access to an online video or some audio
- A sample of a product
- A tips booklet
- A free consultation
- A free service
- Webinars and teleseminars
- A live event
- Some other free information resource, such as a how-to guide
- A workshop or free training session

## Real Life Example

In my salon, we gave away a voucher for a free personal training session. The client brought their own tools into the salon and we taught them how to use them properly to create two to three workable styles at home.

The idea is that you are giving away something valuable in return for something even more valuable to you over time than a sale - their contact details. I cannot stress enough that people are ready to buy when they are ready to buy. In the main, when they hit your page they will either be searching for information, or you will be interrupting them to provide them with information.

Therefore, you need to get their details so you can continue giving them information. Then, when they are ready to buy, you will be at the front of their mind.

When you get your lead to your website, what happens next? The pages are not random. You need to have them follow a particular path. Your website should really have; a Home Page; Terms and Conditions/Privacy Page; a Contact Page and a About Us Page. That's pretty much the maximum. Then you will have very specific and highly-targeted Landing Pages that are not publically published, but are attached to your website, encouraging your leads to take some action.

To tell you what your website and/or landing pages should look like and do, it's easier to go through the mistakes that most websites contain. I will go though each of these in detail and inform you what you need to do in order to rectify them:

1. Lack of purpose or focus

2. Poor design

3. Lack of attention to detail

4. Poor content

5. Lack of overall strategy

All of these things will destroy your response, or the action your want you prospect to take. That is, what you want your lead to do when they hit your page.

## 1. Lack of purpose

Every page must have one purpose. The one purpose is generally to get the prospect to take action (and there should only be one call to action). That action could be one of three things:

i.   Buy something.

ii.  Contact you (if their need is urgent).

iii. Give you information such as an email address or physical address so that you can send them something and start a relationship with them.

The mistake that most websites makes is an ego-boosting show of the owner's talents and skills that they think is 'engaging' or 'informing' the prospect about how talented they are. This is an utter waste of time. Your lead will have a look and move on (in an average of eight seconds). If you are paying for that lead to be on your page through paid advertising, you have just wasted that money. Great for an ego boost but useless for bringing money into your business.

You need to have a strong call to action. Have a really good think about what you are hoping to achieve with your page: is it new business? Is it getting more business from existing clients? Where do you want the business to come from and from whom? How profitable will that business be? (So you know how much you are prepared to spend.) This is all down to your purpose.

The purpose of one of my landing pages is to get people to leave an email address and opt-in to getting the '**33 Ideas to Growing Your Salon FAST**' email follow up sequence and then get them to buy into my Inner Circle and other products.

Another landing page asks people to get a copy of this book by leaving their physical address, then they get the option to also sign up for the '**33 Ideas to Growing Your Salon FAST**' email follow up sequence, and so on. The idea of a person browsing around your site, 'engaging' and then buying from you immediately is a fantasy - a nice fantasy admittedly, but if you believe that's what happens then you are delusional.

If you haven't captured the prospect's attention and got them thinking about their problem and what you might be able to do about it, they will be gone forever. As they also will be if you have links to social media on the page. They are distracting, a waste of space and will ensure that your lead leaves to have a 'look' and then stays on that platform, without returning to your site.

You can have social media links if you must, but have them after the lead has signed up or opted into your free report or email sequence - on the thank you page, for example - then you have their details and they can discover more about you at their leisure.

You should have dedicated landing pages for every specific, highly focused and targeted purpose. If you want someone to join an email sequence regarding hair loss, that landing page should be specifically targeted to and written for hair loss. If you want someone to download a free report regarding highlights, that landing page should be specifically targeted and written for highlights. And so on. You might have dozens of different landing pages, hundreds even, all doing one specific thing and having one specific purpose.

You can do this on any site, even your existing one, without having to redesign it entirely. In fact, for using Google advertising, which I will go into more in this chapter, your landing pages will need to be linked to a main website with a privacy policy, contact and home page anyway.

One final thing regarding purpose. With most online (and offline) advertising you are doing what is called 'interruption advertising'. You are breaking into the prospect's current stream of consciousness and trying to get their attention away from what they are currently doing.

---

Your website and landing pages have to be focused, as they need to work hard to get that attention.

---

## 2. Poor design

If your website designer asks you about how you want your website to look or 'feel' before they ask you about its function or the focus - find someone else or educate them. Always remember that form follows function.

When you know what your website needs to do, you will know what it should look like. If you need further information on the layout of your site, or anything to do with the layout of Direct Response Marketing pieces, check out Colin Wheildon's book, *'Type and Layout: Are you communicating or just making pretty shapes?'* It's a brilliant manual of everything you'll need. But here are some of the basic rules of design:

i. **When it comes to the crunch, it comes down to readability - if it doesn't get read it doesn't get responded to.** If you were taught to read from left to right, then your natural reading habit happens like this when you hit a page: your eyes come to the top right of the page and scan to the left, then they drop down in what is known as reading gravity. So the best place for a picture is right across the top of the page or in the top right hand corner.

ii. **Everything should have a headline, no exceptions.**

iii. **If you have an image or video across the top of the page, then the headline should go below the image or video.** Images pull the eye more strongly than the headline and then the eye 'falls down' with the reading gravity. If you have the headline above the image it is unlikely to be read, which isn't helpful as the headline provides context, so the reader knows exactly what is being said at the outset.

iv. **All images should have a caption (except videos where the caption is implied in the script of the video).** For images across the top, the headline is the caption.

v. **If you are selling a product straight off the page (only for ecommerce websites), the image should be of the product being used, not just the product on its own or the packaging.** Show a 'slice of life', which your prospect can relate to.

vi. **Faces are good images to use to attract attention.** Have the eyes looking out of the page at the reader, but avoid abstract images or stock images of a homogenised group of people.

vii. **The body copy (your message) should be set fully justified - that is straight to the left and right margins.** The first line of each paragraph should be indented. This layout trains the brain instantly to the width of the paragraph, which makes reading seem effortless.

viii. **The font for your online page should be sans serif in general.** Examples are Helvetica, Arial and Univers, but there are many, many more. In offline printing, such as sales letters and postcards, you should use a serif font. Sans serif font online is no longer a hard and fast rule now that screens have higher definition, allowing you to read the fonts more easily and not be pixelated. If in doubt, go with what can be most easily read.

ix. **Font size should be at least 11pt, with 13pt leading (the space between the lines).** If you have an older audience, always go larger with the font size. Older people - myself included - have deteriorating eyesight and need more light to see clearly, making small font a struggle. Make the font big enough to be read comfortably. The font colour should be black or dark grey on a white, ivory or very pale grey background. Do not have an image behind the font in any circumstance. Avoid large blocks of capital text and reverse type (black background with white type) - these will just make it very hard to read. Leave your 'creativity' for inside the salon.

x. **The line length of your copy should be between 20 to 60 characters long (so ideally around 40).** If you have long copy you might want to split it into columns.

xi. **Centralise your headings, but not your body copy.**

xii. **Use subheadings (the same layout as headings),**

**particularly in long copy.** If you do these correctly, people who prefer to scan copy instead of read every word can get the full message from these.

xiii. **Test where you place your video if you have one - across the top or on the left hand side, with an opt-in box on the right.** See which gives you the best response.

xiv. **Test a single column of text against two columns.**

xv. **Have a second opt-in box at the end of any long copy that goes below the bottom of the screen.** Readers are lazy and will not necessarily scroll back to the top to add their details. Make it as easy as possible for them to leave their details.

xvi. **Don't be all things to all visitors.** Where possible, have one focus for each page. This is slightly different if you are selling ecommerce, i.e., just products on your website. But even here you can narrow down the products onto landing pages to just a few of your bestsellers. You can follow up with upsells or cross sales when the client is at the checkout stage. Use your analytics to find out what your clients are doing on your site and then focus on what the top 20% are buying.

xvii. **Video is very powerful, but it's not something you have to do professionally.** Cheap and cheerful videos can work very well. You will have to test it of course to see what response you get, but don't shell out until you see.

### 3. Lack of attention to detail

Spelling mistakes are a problem on printed material, both online and off, as are grammatical errors. If your attention to detail is shit on your website, what will your prospect think of your attention to detail on their most prized possession - themselves - in your salon? Use a second pair of eyes and get a proofreader on everything. If you want to outsource your copy, a good copywriter will pay dividends, but if you can, and you are up for it, it is better to write your own, as nobody knows your business as well as you do.

### Assumptions matter

When you are writing for your prospects, don't assume they know what you are talking about. Spell everything out on their level. If you want to talk about a 't-section', explain exactly what that is. Don't use industry jargon or acronyms without a full explanation. And don't assume they will understand you have a solution for them if you haven't mentioned the problem they have.

Tell them their problems. For example, the pain and frustration they have in trying to get sleek, glossy hair when it is dry and damaged, and how that makes them feel. Then talk about the service or product that will provide the solution of getting well-nourished, moisturised hair and their self-esteem and confidence back.

### Things that don't work

There is nothing more frustrating than an appealing website with broken links, videos that don't play or shopping carts that don't take you through to the checkout. You will not get your desired response if anything on your site is broken or not displaying correctly.

### 4. Poor content

The biggest mistake in your content or body copy is when you focus on the solution and not the problem. Tell your prospect about their problem first and connect their problem to your solution by using the process of AIDA - Attention, Interest, Desire and Action (which I will talk more about in this chapter and beyond). Begin with their problem, which is principally your headline. Don't talk about features, talk about benefits. Tell them why the feature is a benefit, otherwise why would they care? Think about their problem.

### Don't talk about Us, I and We

People don't care about you; they care about their problem. If it is not going to be yourself (and there are reasons you might choose not to), pick a person to be the face of the business. This is to help establish trust and a build a relationship with the prospect. You can't easily do this if you talk about Us and We and a faceless group. Even your *'About'* page shouldn't be all about you and how many awards you won in primary school, it should be 'About' your client's problem and your solutions to it if they sign up.

### Don't be boring

This is a cardinal sin. And anything that begins: *"Hi, and welcome to our website..."* is the kiss of death, and you should be severely punished for even considering it.

### Follow the AIDA formula

Get their Attention with their problem, which you are going to solve, and then establish their Interest by agitating their pain and hinting at your promise of a solution. Now create Desire with your proposition about your promise of being able to solve their problem, provide social proof in the form of testimonials from others who had their problem solved from the same solution, and provide a strong Call to Action with what they need to do in order to get that solution.

Combined with this, your offer is the make or break thing. If your offer is crap it is not going to work. Your offer can be one of many simple things (but only one thing): a free pdf report, a free sample, a free 30-day trial of services, a hardcopy book, a free personalised consultation with a prescriptive product goody bag. Anything that is compelling enough to entice your prospect to give you their details.

### Have a clear style path from entry to exit, and only one call to action.

The prospect needs to have one point of entry into the copy and one clear way to take action. Not a hundred bits of information all over the page, which are all vying for attention and ultimately getting none.

### 5. Lack of strategy

Your website and landing pages must play a part in your overall strategy. They are not a thing out on their own doing all the work. You have to think about how and where the webpage fits within your strategy: what comes next? Where is the prospect going after the webpage? What are you trying to achieve with it?

Remember, strategies work, but tactics (and your webpages are just tactics) sometimes don't. A website doesn't work in isolation. Make sure yours is just another tool in the bigger picture.

Once you have your prospect's details, you don't want them hanging about on your website. You should be controlling the dialogue. It's not a charity or a social club where you provide forums for discussion. Forums are an utter waste of time because they distract from the goal of stimulating sales and end up actually stimulating pointless and petty arguments. Once you have an opt-in from your prospect, your website has served its purpose. Yes, having a website in business is crucial, but only as a tactic to get a relationship started. No more.

*Real Life Example*

**Debunking the myth that you must have your prices on your website.**

Who says? Well, for ecommerce sites it's pretty important to have the price on the product or you are going to have some difficulty getting people to add it to their basket (not impossible, mind you, but it would require more work). But for you in the service industry, having a full list of all your services

- which is not only probably complicated due to all the different levels of staffing, but also huge given all the different services and their combinations - is probably doing your business more damage than good.

Why?

a.  **You get price buyers who are shopping around and comparing you to your competitors based on price alone.** I have actually taken a phone call from a new prospect who said: *"I've been looking at your price for a full head of highlights and it's £75 more expensive than my current hairdresser. Can you match his price?"* WTAF? But before I said that out loud I asked, *"So what is wrong with your current hairdresser that has made you call me?"*

b.  **You limit yourself to set prices which don't incorporate a bespoke service to fit your clients' needs and...**

c.  **You create an expectation of what services 'should' cost, not what the value is to the client.** This proves exceptionally tricky when you want to raise your prices.

I made the decision to take prices off the salon site to test what would happen. Did we lose sales? On the contrary, our telephone enquiry rate increased by 300% and I made sure the staff attempted to convert every enquiry on price into an in-salon consultation and ultimately a purchased service. Test it with yours and see.

## PPC

What is PPC?

Your prospective client is sitting on the sofa, cup of tea in hand, one eye on the TV and the other on the tablet on her lap. She is scrolling through Facebook (for example) and in her newsfeed is a sponsored post that one of her good friends has liked. She is curious and clicks on the ad, which takes her through to your webpage or landing page. If this is your ad, then Facebook will charge you for this Click Through.

Alternatively, your prospective client is surfing the internet looking for the cause of greasy hair. She types, *"Why do you get greasy hair?"* into the Google search bar and a number of links and descriptions pop up in list form. She clicks on a link that says, *"7 secrets to getting rid of greasy hair,"* which happens to be your online ad (your paid listing), and this takes her through to one of your landing pages. Google will then charge you for the Click Through.

This is known as PPC or Pay Per Click advertising. The rules and rates of PPC advertising are specific to each platform (Google, Yahoo, Bing, Facebook, YouTube, etc.), but the basic premise is that you 'bid' for Click Throughs and the rates are determined by the platform's formula, which may include things such as: the competitive nature of your business industry, popular keywords that people use, time of day and probably the colour of your eyes. Well, maybe not the colour of your eyes, but it's a complicated set of rules whereby the platforms make a lot of money.

But you are there to make money too and make money you can. The beauty of PPC advertising is that it is so sophisticated and pervasive that you can be very specific in your targeting and get your ad in front of the person who is likely to want to respond to it. Rather than a scattergun approach, such as a newspaper ad which is priced per cm regardless of how many people read your ad, you only pay for your ad if and when your prospect clicks on it.

---

The trick is getting the right person to click.

---

### Google and Bing

Whilst Google wasn't the first to implement the PPC model, it is probably the first company you will think of in relation to it. Its AdWords tool allows you to place ads on its search engine. However, there are other platforms that use PPC. Bing is a Microsoft-owned search engine and, in an effort to beat Google, Microsoft and Yahoo have combined to provide advertisers an alternative, which is called Bing Ads.

As I've stated above, Google and Bing are search engines, so it should come as no surprise to learn that AdWords and Bing Ads work on search advertising (as opposed to interruption advertising which I will go into in Facebook and LinkedIn advertising). That means people are actively surfing the net looking for a solution to a problem they have, and if your ad comes up, hopefully it means that you can provide that solution.

*AdWords* has traditionally been the main advertising platform for many businesses. But it is a behemoth, and expensive to get wrong. Google will take whatever money you are willing to throw at it, and if you fuck it up it's expensive. People I know who have been using it for years still spend a lot of time on the intricacies of key words and cost per click.

It's a complicated process and if you understand it and are doing well out of it, great. If not, there is the option of outsourcing it to specialised companies (with the proviso that you are constantly on top of them when it comes to results), or just picking something else to start with that is going to give you less headaches and a better ROI.

I personally have spent time on Google and it took ages to get it right. (I've spent a similar amount of time on Facebook and so far it's easier, and gives me better quality leads). There is a huge amount of information available out there on Google AdWords mastery. Google itself will also help you out with a dedicated manager if you desire (just be aware that the notion of 'helpful service' is a bit free and loose when it comes to these guys), so I am not going to go into it in massive detail here.

What do the ads look like? When I started writing this book the Google ads appeared at the top of your search results, handily signposted by the little yellow 'ad' icon, and down the right hand side. Bing ads looked almost identical, except you also got ads at the bottom of your page of search results too. The ads consisted of a clickable headline, a URL beneath it, then one or two lines of text, depending on how you had your campaign ads set up.

You could also get different links at the bottom of your ad. A few weeks later, Google ads completely changed, with nothing on the right hand side, and their ads appeared at the top and bottom of the search results. Bing had changed as well. This is a great example of how you have no control over how your tactics work, and why you shouldn't just rely on one.

Google and Bing are constantly changing their rules, T&Cs and algorithms, so you have to keep a close eye on what they are doing. The only thing you have control over is putting the time and effort into identifying what your target audience is likely to be searching for.

You can do this using Google's free Keyword Tool, which will tell you what phrases and words people are searching for, how much competition there is for certain keywords, and how often people are searching for them. It's a lot of info and as I've already said, it may pay to get a professional involved before your money is sucked into the Google drain, to ensure your ROI is what you want it to be.

*Bing* is more relaxed at the moment about what you can and can't do with its adverts, and it's also much cheaper (that could change though). As a side note to that, if you do fall foul of Google's many rules and regulations for ad creation (and there are many and they change regularly without much notice), you may well be 'Google slapped' and your account will be suspended. I've heard from people who've been there, it's a shit position to be in and you want to avoid it at all costs. Play nice and work out what the rules are so you don't get into Google's bad books. Just saying.

It's a good idea to run ads on Bing to test them out and see how they perform before moving on to AdWords. Bing has a much smaller platform and user base, which is why it's cheaper, but it's also useful to discover which ads are likely to work well.

## Analytics

Regardless of whether you are using AdWords PPC or not, you should sign up to Google Analytics. This data-gathering machine allows you to compare your online campaigns to check which yield the most traffic and conversions (sales). You can find out where your best visitors are located, see what people are specifically searching for on your site, or find out when they abandon the shopping cart (if ecommerce). These are all things that will help you fix errors and become more focused in your targeting. Google Analytics is huge on data, as you can imagine, and you can find yourself wading through it forever.

**Therefore, to make things a bit easier for you, the most important areas you will need to look at are:**

1. **Visitor numbers** - so you can measure your lead generation strategies (another reason to have specific traffic driven to specific landing pages).

2. **Traffic sources** - so you can see where your leads are coming from and which landing pages are working for you.

3. **Goals (conversion)** - so you can see what's happening once traffic hits your site.

All of this is important stuff that will enable you to get more sophisticated with your campaigns and optimise your ROI.

## A note on SEO

I haven't gone into the subject of SEO (Search Engine Optimisation), whereby you try to get your ad listing to the top of

Google by organic means, i.e., without paying for ads. This is because, in the main, it is a shit way to get traffic and the results you get are out of your control. The results aren't reliable, they're not scalable and they are unfocused and unmeasurable. Plus, the traffic you get from it is unqualified and generally low quality (browsers not buyers). In addition to all of that, if that is not enough for you, SEO is a lot of work for little return and Google can and does change its algorithm overnight.

A real life example of this comes from a business owner friend of mine who used SEO solely for his traffic source. He had great success for a number of years but then Google changed the algorithm concerning how it prioritises SEO ads, and overnight his business was wiped out. It's not a secure way to advertise. What you can do is make sure your meta tags (special codes that are added to your website that describe some aspect of the content and are important for search engines robots when they are picking up information to show the searcher) and posts are tagged correctly so that at least they show up on a natural search.

This is another example of prioritising your efforts with the 80/20 Principle. 80% of your focus should be getting paid for and targeted leads. If you get some leads through SEO then great, but don't spend a lot of time trying to get them through this method.

## YouTube

When hanging out on YouTube, your prospect is also in the 'search' frame of mind.

Google-owned YouTube uses the Google AdWords platform for its advertising area. So you will need to have an AdWords account as well as a YouTube one. At present, there are four types of YouTube ads (although yes, this may change).

1. **Display ads appear on the right hand side of the feature video and above the video suggestions, on the desktop platform only.**

2. **Overlay ads are those semi-transparent ads that appear overlaid on the bottom 20% of your video.** These are also only available on the desktop platform.

3. **Skippable video ads allow you to skip the ad after five seconds of pre-roll.** These can pop up before, during, or after the main video on desktops, mobile devices, TV and games consoles.

4. **Non-skippable video ads and long, non-skippable video ads are compulsory viewing: your viewer has to watch them before they can watch the main video.** Long ones can be up to 30 seconds, and they can pop up before, during, or after the main video. These are available on desktop and mobile devices.

The ads themselves are easily identifiable from the little yellow 'Ad' icon, the same as in Google search results.

YouTube ads can be good value, as you are only paying for the ad after the five seconds of pre-roll are up. If the viewer decides to 'skip this ad' you don't pay, but you get five seconds of free PR! Create a video advert that has a very strong image or message that talks to your target audience. You can then attach it to many different sectors of your target market. You then only pay when that target market watches beyond the first five seconds of pre-roll. The clever thing that YouTube has introduced is a click through link on the video that takes your lead off the video and onto your webpage.

The same rules of advertising apply here: follow the AIDA (Attention, Interest, Desire, Action) principle and remember it is still a form of interruption advertising. You still have to solve the prospect's problems and get them off the page. Make sure you have a call to action. This is not about pretty images making you 'feel' something. The ads need to do the work of getting your prospect to 'do' something.

You don't have to have a professionally-shot video with all the bells and whistles. A cheap and cheerful job filmed on a smartphone can also get results. Test it first and then build it up. What you want is for the Attention and Interest to be created from the video so you can lead them to Desire and Action on your follow up web or landing page.

And if you haven't tried it yet, bear in mind that YouTube gets more searches than Google these days...

## Banner ads and remarketing

Banner Ads appear all over the internet, so much so that experts say that people don't really see them anymore, that your brain has become inured to them. They are ads that appear on a webpage (for example, your favourite online news like *The Daily Mail*) as a large box across the top of the page, or as a smaller box in the text down the right hand side. They may not get as noticed as much anymore, but the cool thing is your ads will appear when prospects are looking at their favourite webpages, and you have a loose association with those pages and the content in them. Playing with the big boys so to speak. But the real beauty in them now is that you can use them in your long-term strategy of relentless follow up with remarketing campaigns.

Remarketing is where you place a pixel (piece of code) on your web page that tracks visitors. When someone has looked at your page the pixel follows them onto whatever pages they look at and your banner ad is served up to them again and again, like a fixated stalker. This is a long-term game as you are unlikely to get a lot of click-throughs on these ads, but you get a lot of free exposure as you 'follow' your prospect around the internet. This means you will be more familiar to your prospect, and they will feel like they have a relationship with you already.

There are loads of ways you can set these ads up, but probably the easiest and simplest method is to use Google's Display Network ads. They show your ads to past website visitors when they visit other websites in Google's Display Network.

**You can also do other clever stuff, as follows:**

1. **Dynamic remarketing.** Amazon does this a lot. Have you ever looked at a product on Amazon, then wandered off – only to see ads for that Amazon product everywhere you go? TripAdvisor and other travel companies also use this tool to great effect. That's dynamic remarketing.

2. **Remarketing for mobile app.** Here you can show ads to people who have used your mobile app or visited your mobile website, when they use other mobile apps or websites.

3. **Remarketing lists for search ads.** You can show ads to people who've left your website but are now doing follow up searches on Google.

4. **Video remarketing.** These ads get shown to people who've watched your videos or browsed your YouTube channel, when they go elsewhere on YouTube or watch other videos on Display Network sites.

And the beauty is, you only need to set up the remarketing once and it chugs on relentlessly doing the work for you.

## Facebook

I want to stress that I am talking about Facebook advertising, as opposed to Facebook page 'likes' and engagement, which mean absolutely nothing. The difference is:

Ads can be tested, measured and scaled up or down, 'likes' cannot.

Got that into your head? Good. Let's begin…

Unlike Google and Bing, Facebook is interruption marketing in that people are not specifically searching for a thing while on this platform. With interruption marketing, you have to appeal to the pain the lead has, without them searching for it. When you are spending time on Facebook yourself, you are not necessarily searching for a solution to a problem you have. You are probably a bit hypnotically challenged: just looking at pretty pics and reading inane comments. So when an ad or suggested/sponsored post pops up on your feed, you will look at it if it appeals to some pain point you might have. It works for your leads the same way. You will be taking them from a point of being 'social' - reading posts from their friends and others - and interrupting them with something they weren't planning on looking at.

So your ad has to resonate with them enough for them to click on it and move away from whatever they were doing. And this is important. You need to take them off Facebook and onto your landing page so that you can get them to do the thing you want (opt-in to a free report or email sequence) and start a relationship with them. It's ideal if you can make your landing page look very similar to where they have just come from. That way it won't jolt their senses and make them want to click away.

On the premise that you have set up your website's opt-in box and your follow up sequence, you'll be wanting to drive traffic to your webpage to get new, qualified prospects onto your list. For example, if you have niched in wedding hair and you are looking to attract new business, one great source of traffic is Facebook.

Targeting newly-engaged women is a great way to get your message in front of the person who is going to make the buying decision. Let me make this very clear; you are not looking to boost posts or get engagement through 'LIKES' - that is NOT going to get you business in any way that is scalable or measurable, and it is a waste of your time. I'm talking about using Facebook's paid adverts platform.

Given that there are over three billion users of Facebook worldwide, you have a pretty good chance of the right person seeing your ad and responding to it. Again, keep in mind that Facebook advertising is interruption advertising. When your ads are served up by Facebook, your prospect is not looking for a product or service; they're doing something else (swiping past yet another motivational photo of a gratuitous sunset, or 'liking' cute animal videos, or something equally inane). So, when you are setting up your ads you need to get their attention away from what mindset they are in and into a position of being interested in your solution to their problem, especially given that they didn't know they had that problem until your ad popped up.

Images in ads are the key here. This is much more so for Facebook than for many other advertising or lead generation platforms, because it's a visual medium. Choose your images carefully and either alternate them or change them often. If not, your audience will experience 'ad fatigue' and your click rate will drop-off, as they will become oblivious having seen it too often. Images that do well are faces, particularly babies, children or pretty young women - all looking at the camera. But you will need to test your images for your niche and tweak them as necessary. Therefore, keep a stock of images and alternate them for the ad.

Once you have your image and headline sorted, you'll need to think about the client you want to target. Generally, start broader than you want to end up. For example, in the corporate niche, begin with men and women aged over 34 who are married and own a business. Get yourself a thousand or so opt-ins, then trawl through the data to see what else you can find out about them. You might find a high percentage of them are a certain age group, or have similar interests.

There's one guy I heard about who ran an online dating/mail-order bride site. After doing a bit of research he found out his biggest clients all had one thing in common - they were predominately long-haul truck drivers. So he tailored his message and changed his whole website to target that audience specifically.

You will find something of your own that will let you target sign-ups more precisely. Then you set up a whole new group of ads aimed at a much narrower audience. You'll get fewer clicks but it's more likely that they will be higher quality leads, and therefore you'll have higher conversions to buying your product or service.

The key is to get them off Facebook and onto your landing page, so your link on your ad should always be getting them away from Facebook and the mindset of 'that's interesting' to the mindset of 'they are trying to give me information about a solution to my problem, I'm really interested'.

**For now Facebook ads appear in two places:**

1. **In your newsfeed.** Ads that appear here have a higher chance of getting noticed and therefore clicked on. You'll need a Facebook page to have your ads served up on your target's newsfeed. They are called 'sponsored posts' as opposed to a straight 'advert'. Setting up a page for your business is relatively simple.

2. **On the right-hand side.** This is not the best place to be, as you won't get noticed as much. People know they are adverts and ignore them more. You want to get your ads into the newsfeed as much as you can.

**I've used Facebook advertising and had great success. The benefits are:**

- ✔ **The ads can be targeted to a specific audience (you can target a list of clients you already have by uploading their email addresses into 'custom audience').**

- ✔ **It's not too expensive (yet).**

- ✔ **It's easy to measure.** Tracking codes are available through a Facebook pixel on your webpage and you can measure the effectiveness of your advert by looking at the number of people clicking on it, going through to your webpage, clicking through and then downloading your free report or opting into your emails. Simple.

## LinkedIn

LinkedIn ads are a similar platform to Facebook ads, but they tend to be a better method for selling to businesses. It is after all, a business platform. The cost of advertising on LinkedIn is higher than advertising on Facebook and your Click Through Rate (CTR) will be lower, but the leads you'll get will probably be of a better quality. It's likely that this is because of the type of people using LinkedIn and the mindset they are in when using it (predominately business).

**You can put your ads in three different places:**

1. **On the right hand side.** There are two types: banner ads and PPC ads. Banner ads are large, flexible and have the bonus of showing up to 30 seconds of video content. Therefore they are the more expensive of the two. PPC ads are much like the ones you see on Facebook: A headline, an image and some text.

2. **Newsfeed ads.** Does what it says on the tin. Ads in your newsfeed. They are often called 'sponsored content'.

3. **Text link ads.** A hyperlinked headline that appears at the top of your LinkedIn page. When a prospect clicks on this ad it takes them straight to your landing page. Text link ads are no-frills ads.

Just like Facebook, the key is targeting. Get your targeting right and your ads will do much better. LinkedIn is also like Facebook in that it stores masses of data about its users and you can use that to be very specific about whom you want as a potential client.

## Chapter 9. Summary

→ **Tactics are the tools or medium you use to get your message to your prospective clients.** They are the short-term implementation of your long-term strategy.

→ **No one tactic is the right or only way for you to get your message across.** You can and should use multiple platforms.

→ **There are many online advertising platforms with which to digitally advertise your service.** Your goal is to find out where your ideal client hangs out, so that you can get your message in front of them.

→ **Your website exists solely to capture leads.** It's not an ego-boosting 'look at my creative stuff'. It's not about you, it's about your prospect's problem and how you might be able to solve it.

→ **The key to using online advertising is targeting.** If you have taken action in Chapter 3 and created your Ideal Client Avatar, you can start tailoring your advertising to them.

### Take Action

Take a good look at your website and see if it conforms to any of the elements I have written about in this chapter. Does it capture leads? If not, overhaul it now.

## CHAPTER TEN

# OFFLINE ADVERTISING – PRINT IS NOT DEAD

## Offline Advertising

What is it?

Although you may think that the internet and all its convenience means that print is dead, that is far from true. There are big rewards to be had from a great offline campaign. And when I talk about offline marketing, I am mostly referring to printed material and direct mail.

**Why? There are a number of reasons:**

- **Fewer people do it, and it's one way to get noticed in a crowded environment. But only if you do it correctly, of course.**

- **It has a higher perceived value than online tactics, probably because we see printed material as more permanent.**

- **A piece of direct mail will sit around someone's home or office for an average of 17 days, so it's like a 17-day follow up.**

- **The experience of receiving direct mail stops you in your tracks.** Don't underestimate the power of print media in a digital world. Generation Y and the Millenials have missed out on a lifetime of getting something in the post, and they will be sure to open something because it is now a novelty.

---

The challenges of offline marketing such as direct mail are: Getting it opened; Getting it read.

---

Your offer is worth diddlysquat if your prospect just bins it without so much as a cursory glance. But there are ways and means to increase the 'open rate' of your hard work, which I will go into later. First, let's look at some examples. That is, sending out printed material to prospects. Unlike email marketing, where it is a cardinal sin to buy a mailing list from a third party, you can get pretty good lists for direct mail. It is not a sin (because these are lists where people have agreed to get information from third parties) and if your offer, package and targeting are good, you can get great results.

## Postcards

Once you have your targeted direct mail list you would do well to start with a postcard providing a snippet of information about your prospect's problem and what you can do for them when they respond to your offer. Even though it is a snippet it should contain all the requirements of a good piece of copy and the AIDA principle. Make sure you have a compelling headline, create interest by acknowledging their problem, show that you can solve it and let them know what they should do now to get that information.

A5 or A6 postcards are a cheap, cheerful and easy-to-produce way of getting your message out there. They are not used enough so they also have a unique quality. Another plus point is that they are 'keepable', meaning people can stick them on their fridges or on their noticeboards if you put useful information on them. Your offer can be as simple as just getting them to go to your webpage and opt-in in order to receive your free report or email sequence, or to call you to redeem something. Have a tracking code with your offer that the prospect has to quote in response.

Just remember to put your full message on both sides of the postcard, because there's no such thing as Side 1 and Side 2. There's only The Side That Your Prospect Sees First. I've included a great example from my friend Mo who owns a very successful promotional products company, Club Row Creations. This one works really well for him to get lapsed clients to buy again. (Printed with permission).

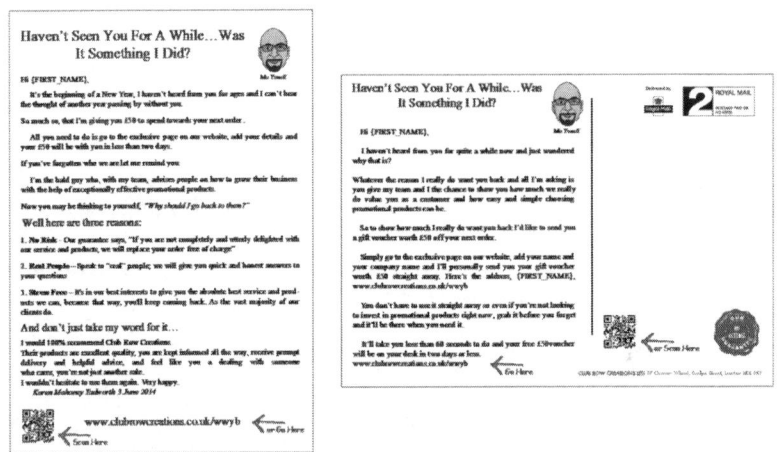

*Figure 2. Mo's awesome "Is it something I did?" postcard.*

## Sales letters

Writing a sales letter is quite hard work. To craft a good letter that will get a good response from new leads is a big ask, and it can take hours of work and years of practice. You have to work to create a brand new relationship with someone and persuade them to like and trust you, and then take action by buying your thing.

Sales letters are best used after you have started a relationship with your prospects, and a great place to begin is after you have sent out a postcard, as outlined above. The letter will take the form of a longer version of the story. Sales letters work best when you have a product launch or very specific offer, and long copy usually does better than short.

An info-marketing guy I know got stupendous results with a 32-page letter, but you will have to test to see what works best for you. A sales letter should cover what you know about the prospect's problem and the pain they have, show them the solution you can provide with your product or service, tell them how they can get it and what happens when they buy it, and then some proof about how it has worked for others. A sales letter is not all about the features of the 'thing'.

**There are some general rules about how to put together a powerful sales letter - it's not just a random ramble of thoughts, the letter should follow the following sequence, which will encourage your prospect to actually read it:**

1. **Open with a powerful, compelling, interesting and persuasive headline.**

2. **Tell the full story.** If you were talking to the prospect face-to-face, you would take the time to tell the full story of the benefits, advantages and reasons why of your product or service. Do the same with your sales letter.

3. **Write as you speak.** Use everyday language and avoid industry jargon and acronyms.

4. **Have your ideal client avatar in mind and think about what their hopes, dreams and fears are.** You are writing to their problem. Be them. If you can connect with someone in this way and show them that your solution solves their problem, they will be more compelled to trust you and buy from you.

5. **Include a compelling call to action.** Make sure it is specific and easy to follow.

6. **Include a P.S. (Postscript.)**

7. **Include your signature.**

Send your letter out in a handwritten addressed envelope (printers can produce handwritten fonts and printing that looks pretty much like the real thing if you have hundreds and don't want writer's cramp) and put a real stamp on it, not a preprinted frank. The more it looks like a personal piece of mail and not another sales piece, the more likely it is to be opened. You can get creative with this too. One web designer I know individually handwrote a little booklet that folded up into its own envelope (similar to an aerogramme). She got a great response, and a 100% open rate, as it was such a unique piece of mail in her list's post boxes.

But no matter how good your letter, the impact is not in sending it out on its own and waiting for the sales to roll in, consider it as something that goes with other direct mail as part of a system. And as an added note here, to say that we know that a set sales letter will work in getting a client in the door is a fallacy, a single cause fallacy. And that applies to all tactics of marketing.

---

## No one thing is the way.

---

We can make educated predictions on why one ad, or one sales letter will work better than others based on the general rules of DRM. But if someone is telling you there is only one way like those that peddle NLP, or Social Media Marketing or The Secret, run a mile.

## Bulky mail

Have you ever had post delivered and noticed a little package amongst all the flyers and bills? Not only will it have instantly captured your attention, but what did you open first, the bills or the lumpy package? Bulky mail is a great way to ensure that your prospective client is at least opening your message. And once opened, the lumpy part of the package - usually a branded gift, something intriguing or of high-perceived value (not just a ballpoint pen with your logo on it) - will help pique the recipient's interest and hopefully make them want to read your sales message on what their problem is and how you can provide a solution to it.

There is a dual benefit to bulky mail. Not only does it guarantee you a better open rate, and therefore a better response rate compared to a plain letter, the promotional product you put inside it can also be seen by everyone they come into contact with, so it's additional exposure and additional advertising, without having to spend more money. And if the product is quirky enough, your prospect is going to show it to others. I guarantee there are very few, if any, salons that do this. And when people talk, they will say, *"my hairdresser does..."* And that's gold.

A friend of mine, the aforementioned Mo, runs a promotional products business and is really successful at it. Promotional products are not just for big corporates. And the products themselves don't have to be boring. In fact, Mo runs a campaign called *'Challenge Mo',* where he dares his clients to ask him to find the most bizarre items to print their messages on. I've used him to source handbag-sized pop-out brushes, gold peppermints and green shower caps. The choice is only limited by your imagination. Mo has printed on penis pumps, horse blankets, camouflage-coloured toilet roll and condoms. Nope, nothing boring there. Just use whatever you think your prospect will respond to.

Of course, you also need to think about the message you give with the product. What will you have printed on it? Your logo and a contact, a message that is congruent with your sales letter and/or your call to action? For example, you could have a boomerang with your website details and a message that reads, *"we miss you and just like a boomerang we want you back,"* which is targeted at non-returning clients. Make it relevant and fun.

And here is something even deeper. In his book, *'Influence: The Psychology of Persuasion',* Robert Cialdini says that one of the rules of persuading people is by the law of reciprocity, whereby if you do something for someone or give someone something, they generally feel compelled to do something in return.

Think about the pop-up stands in supermarkets on any given weekend, the ones where they hand out free samples. After engaging with them do you feel more obliged to buy the product?

You'll probably feel a bit uncomfortable taking the piece of cheese or whatever it is on offer, eating it, handing back an empty toothpick and walking away. Generally you may stop and ask more about it, even if you don't buy. But the law of reciprocity says it is more likely that you will return the favour by buying the cheese or sausage or chocolate. It works. Otherwise they wouldn't be paying someone to stand all day slicing cheese into slivers and binning used toothpicks with a smile on their face.

If a prospect receives a gift from you, it's quite likely that they will want to do something for you in return. If you have primed them with your call to action (after telling them how you can solve their pain), they are more likely to pick up the phone or book online, or whatever it is that you have asked them to do.

## Print advertising

These are pretty similar to online ads really, in that they follow the same principles: targeting is everything. Pick your publication carefully if you are advertising in newspapers and magazines. Remember to think beyond the obvious. If you are in the wedding hair business, don't just look at Bride magazine, as you will get lost in the plethora of other wedding hair ads. Instead look at niche magazines, such as Women's Health and Fitness; you will be the only one there. And yes, brides do look at this magazine too.

Don't waste your money on ads that look like ads either. Fight your designer and your publication to produce an ad that will actually get read. If it looks like an ad in a magazine your target audience will skim past it at best, ignore it completely at worst. This isn't the result you are looking for, or are paying for. However, if you make your ad look like an article in the publication, with a similar look and layout, also known as an advertorial, the chances of creating interest and of it being read will be much higher.

And that's what you want, because if it gets read it's more likely that it will be responded to. Aside from that, all the usual rules about ads apply: have a strong call to action, a good offer, have your goals in mind and follow up.

## Book

Oh yes, that old chestnut. The book that you will write because no one has done it, the one that will immediately bring you expert status. Your book is an offline tactic like no other, simply because of the gravitas it holds. We, as humans, have a deep respect for the written word in book form, probably as it used to be the domain of a very few elite who could write. And we haven't lost that sense of awe and wonder when someone says, *"I've written a book, I'm a published author."*

By writing a book on a subject you automatically become the expert.

In the sharky-shark world of selling, a book also gives you the opportunity to present yourself and your 'story' in a non-threatening way. Your book takes on the role of educating and informing your prospect, and although it is a sales piece because it will follow all the AIDA principles, it will be more acceptable to your prospect than a hard direct sell. It will give you a USP for your salon if you haven't been able to find one, as it will provide you with a 'hook to hang your business on'. You will become the salon owner who 'wrote that book', and that will give you a leg up into getting yourself in front of the media and ultimately in front of your prospects.

Remember, you're the expert with the book now. You're not just another salon owner and you're no longer in competition with anyone else because you have differentiated yourself from them. You are *educating* your prospects while your competitors are *selling* to them. As a result you can leave your so-called competitors to watch each other, which ultimately means they will be tied into competing on price.

Note that the purpose of writing is not to become a bestselling author and wealthy off the back of its sales and spinoffs. That's a nice gig if you can get it, but thousands of manuscripts move across editors' and publishers' desks every day without ever seeing the printer's ink. But for all the above reasons, your book is a fantastic tool in your marketing belt, so use it to its full effect, ad nauseam.

You can test it by selling it to existing clients as an educational tool, or as something they can show to their friends to get referrals. It's a very powerful way to cement your relationship with your clients, put a ring around them and keep them in your herd. But where it does the heavy lifting is in lead generation to get new clients. If you write it in your own words with your own personality shining through, you will immediately break through that barrier of establishing trust.

Anyone who reads your book should feel that they know you.

If they know you and like what they read, they will like you. And if they like you they will be more likely to buy from you.

**So what do you do with your book after you've written, published and had it printed?**

- **Send it out to journalists with a covering letter attached so they can review it for their magazine/blog/ newspaper/radio station.** When I did this for '*101 Naked Confessions*', I got a diverse set of responses, ranging from a radio station in Melbourne, Australia, to a magazine in Toronto, Canada and a lifestyle blog in Dublin, Ireland.

- **Give it away for free at networking events as your very flash 'business card'.**

- **Put a copy in a new client goody bag.**

- Offer free copies for other industry or charity events for their goody bags.

- Approach local bookstores (not the big chains) to see if they will stock it for you for free in return for all the profits.

- Advertise online for free chapter downloads, with an immediate upsell option to buy the rest.

- Sell it on Amazon.

- Create a Kindle version or other ebook format.

- Record it as an audio book.

- Offer to write for an industry or other magazine, and use chunks of your book as content.

- Give it away to existing clients with referral cards inside, which they can give to their friends, family, colleagues and clients.

- **You may have clients and friends who are in complementary industries** - tanning, wedding planners, event managers, hotels... Give them copies of your book so they can give them to their clients.

And so on.

Once you have all of this going on you can get really jiggy with it and test the following methods:

1. Giving the book away but charging post and packaging.

2. Selling the book at full cost with free shipping.

3. Selling the book with a time-limited discount and free shipping.

4. Doing 2 or 3 with an immediate upsell to paid-for membership to a service or product.

5. Offering a free monthly newsletter with an upsell to the book.

6. Offering a Kindle version of the book with an upsell to the paper version.

7. Offering a paper version of the book with an upsell to the Kindle version.

The list is endless and as long as you are marketing ethically and testing and measuring, you will find your optimal method of lead generation in terms of ROI.

And the beauty of a book as opposed to other forms of offline advertising is that in the majority of cases you only have to write it once. So get cracking.

## Networking

Networking can be exhausting and time-consuming, with relatively little return on your investment of time and energy. I went to many networking events before I knew better and although everyone was friendly and wanted to know about my business, I can count on my hand how many ended up as clients.

If you enjoy networking, pick speciality events and tailor your message to them. Attend them with a purpose in mind: to collect details from willing prospects so that you can add them to your list and relentlessly follow up with them. The quality of the networking attendees for your niche should give you a good idea of which event is going to be worth the hassle of stepping outdoors for, or whether your time would be better spent crafting an ad to get new clients through your door.

Your book - you know that book you wrote way back when you were *Positioning Yourself As The Expert* - is your business card. And what a business card! How many salon owners do you know who have written a book? Not very many, I bet. Is this going to set you apart from your competitors? Hell, yeah. Is it going to get you remembered by people? How will they forget? Especially if you are at a networking event handing out a little pink copy of *'101 Naked Confessions of a Gay Hairdresser!'*

## Referrals

In a salon, referrals are the number one thing that has a phenomenal return on investment. The investment can be as little as asking a client to refer you to their friends and family. The client mentions it, the friend or family member comes in, you wow them and they become a lifelong client. The thing is, most salon owners don't even ask the question, and if they do, it's a passing comment once every six months.

I will bet that you have new clients walking through the door who say, *"Mrs X sent me, or Mr B said you were good."* Feels great to know that people have been talking about you, doesn't it? And it gives you a potential life-long client. But it's random and you have had no influence or control over it at all. Now imagine that you have formalised the process of referrals: regularly asking for them, following them up, giving out incentives for them and tracking them? Can you see how much more this is going to grow your business?

I fucking hope so.

What do I mean by formalise? This is to turn the way you get clients to refer you to others into a process that everyone in the salon can follow. It starts with the question: *"If you like us and like what we do can you please tell others about us? We rely on referrals to keep our business going and it would really help us if you could send people our way."* Make this a priority question either straight after each service, when talking on the phone to someone who is making an appointment, or when you email a client. If asking is a little bit taxing, write it down and send it in a personalised card.

## Real Life Example

In my salon, around 75% of new clients came from referrals. The staff asked the question, but when they forgot, as they were wont to do if we didn't remind them enough, we had a back up in the form of a referral card. This was the size of two business cards and was serrated down the middle. One card said YOURS, the other said THEIRS. There was a call to action to book an appointment by phone or email. The YOURS was the card the existing client kept, the THEIRS was the card they could tear off and give to a friend or family member.

On the YOURS card it said something along the lines of: *"Share this card and you will get £30 off your next visit after your friend has come in".* On the THEIRS side it said: *"Your friend loves you enough to share us with you, bring this card in and get £30 off your first visit".* Then we got a load printed and handed them out like sweets, not just one to each client, handfuls of them, new and existing.

And guess what? The referrals just kept rolling in. And the clients kept asking for more cards to give away as they were getting something out of it, and the new referrals were also in on it and taking cards to give to others.

Now don't make the mistake of thinking you have to give money off a service as an incentive. We also used things like *"Lunch for two at the local Italian restaurant."* You can ask local businesses to donate something so you both get the benefit, or get high street vouchers or cinema tickets - whatever you think your clients are going to be motivated by. In the beginning, I also incentivised our reception staff to remember to give out the cards until it became a habit. When they saw the cards come back in with a new client or an existing one, they too would get a little thrill. Win win.

P.S. Who are your clients going to refer? People who are like them, of course. Very rarely will you get someone who is referred to you who doesn't fit with your ideal client. Why? Because we hang out with people we like, and we will share the things we enjoy with the people we like and who are like us. Sharing your salon with your best friend is quite a compliment.

## Chapter 10. Summary

→ **Print is not dead.** Offline advertising can work just as effectively as online advertising, and sometimes it can work even better, depending on your target audience. The holy grail is a combined offline-online alternating and systemised campaign.

→ **The challenge with offline advertising is getting it opened and getting it read.**

→ **Printed material has a higher perceived value than online advertising, so it is more likely to be responded to.**

→ **Postcards, sales letters, bulky mail, print advertising, books, networking and referrals are all great examples of offline advertising that you can put into place fairly easily.**

### Take Action

Choose an offline medium listed in this chapter and get stuck in. Whether that's formalising your referral system or starting to write your book (more details about how to write your book can be found in Appendix II).

# CHAPTER ELEVEN
# EMAIL MARKETING – THE GOLDEN @

This is my ultimate favourite topic and the most über-profitable tactic of all. Daily emails. These are much maligned by people who either have no idea about them, have never tried them or who have and got it wrong. Daily emails have the dual benefit of building a relationship with your clients (your list) and making you sales. And with a bit of practice and tungsten-tipped balls, they are easy and fun to write.

Email marketing is one of the most effective and powerful ways to make money there is. And at the time of writing this, it's one of the most cost-effective ways of getting business. If done correctly, this one tactic (as long as the foundations of your strategy are set in place) will make you shitloads of money.

**Here are the myths about writing daily emails:**

1. **They are spam.** They are not. Every person who is on your email list should be there by their own agreement, because they signed up for them (and for double protection, oo-er, they have double opted in). Spam consists of unwanted emails that you never signed up for, and they are usually impersonal, ugly and full of photos you can't see with offers that are of no value to you. Interestingly, you are more likely to be considered spam if you only email occasionally and your client is not expecting anything from you.

2. **Nobody wants to be emailed every day.** Nobody wants to be emailed boring, sales emails every day. You'd have to be a very special person to enjoy that. But when your emails are not about your thing (service or product), and are interesting and entertaining, your clients will look forward to your email every day. When I was writing emails as Terry for the salon,

I would have people say that they would stop everyone in the office to read them out each day, or make a cup of tea and have a slice of cake as they enjoyed them. Or they told me how they really looked forward to coming back from a lunch break at 2pm and having an email waiting for them to kick start their afternoon.

3. **You'll lose clients through unsubscribes.** You will lose people through unsubscribes, yes. But if you are sending interesting, informative emails with a call to action the way I do, those who are unsubscribing are not your ideal clients anyway (go back to the chapter on your ideal client). You'll have a few who will unsubscribe because they don't have time or would rather not get a daily email, but will still remain your client. That's absolutely fine. They can be sold to through other media.

4. **People don't like to be sold to.** Everyone likes to be sold to if it's done the right way. Nasty, boring, *"buy my shit for 80% off right now"* is not the right way. Alternatively, seductive selling to people to meet their wants and desires through entertaining and informing them (are you getting the drift yet?) via email is a soft-sell that, when you get it right, will have your clients thanking you for the sale.

5. **I have nothing to write about.** Well, actually, you have everything to write about. Your life as a business owner is not that boring. There will be anecdotes about your days in business, your opinions on national events, a scandalous conversation at a dinner party, seven reasons why your cat reminds you of your mother-in-law, your number one secret as a kid that you have never shared until now, five things you hate and why. Anything and everything is fair game when writing a daily email.

6. **I can't write well.** I'm on many email lists of people who send out daily emails to their clients, similar to the QBofE way. Some of them are extremely articulate and funny, some

are full of typos and fucks, some are short, some take a full cup of coffee to get through. The thing is, everyone can write.

You just have to remember the golden rule - 'write like you speak'.

When you start emailing your list, make sure you tell them you are going to be sending them daily emails and that they will be entertaining and informative and will include an offer. Also tell them that they have an option to unsubscribe from the very beginning, and let them know how to unsubscribe.

Daily emails are stories, but stories that have a very specific structure to them - they are designed to do some work for you. And they are the easiest tactic to use to be relentless in your follow up. Don't get me wrong, you could probably get similar results if you were sending out a printed postcard every single day to your clients, but emails, for now, are fast and effective. And once you get over the apprehension and enjoy the process, you should be able to bang one out in 20 minutes or less, and still have clients asking for more.

## Email Structure, Content And Style

Daily emails have a set structure. Their job is to do the work of a sales page, albeit in a shorter amount of time. Therefore, the principles of selling and AIDA come into play. First and foremost, you want to capture the recipient's *Attention*.

You know how many emails you receive each day, so your one needs to be sticking a flag up and waving furiously in the midst of the other boring stuff that comes in. When the recipient has opened your email, you want to instantly grab their *Interest* so that they start to read. You create *Desire* in the body copy of the email and then have a *Call To Action* towards the end, as well as in the P.S.

So, starting from the top of the email down, here's how you should structure it. There are no hard and fast rules here - each writer will have their own style of writing - but the principles are universal:

### From 'name'

This must be your name, or the name of the person the email is coming from (if you are writing them for someone else). Do not use the company name or the salon name. You are writing person-to-person. If you see a person's name in the 'from' box, you are more likely to be curious and open it.

### Subject line

Your subject line is what is going to get you noticed in the mass of emails that your client receives each day. So, you want to make sure it is *attention*-grabbing but not in the way that Viagra sellers promise you a permanent erection and a string of willing partners. The purpose of the subject line is to entice the client to open the email.

Examples of subject lines from emails I've written are: *"She keeps her hairbrush in a shoebox"*, *"Spandex, sequins and a flowing cape"*, *"Take a pencil and shove it"*, and, *"An itch you have to scratch."* These are all enough to create a tease, to make people wonder exactly what I am talking about and open the email.

### First few lines

After the salutation, where you can have the name of your client auto-filled to personalise it, you start your story. This should be nothing to do with your product or service or thing, but the story that pays out the subject line in the first few lines. The purpose of the first few lines is to get the client to read the next paragraph. For example, with *"An itch you have to scratch,"* the email opened: *"You know that feeling when you want something really badly? Not just think it might be nice. But you've convinced yourself that you want it, and you absolutely must have it. And you will do anything to get exactly what you want. And are you going to settle for a compromise and be sold into something else? No you are not.*

*Why?*

*Because you know that you will be disappointed and you want to satisfy that 'need' emotion that you have a craving for. Nothing feels better than getting what you want. Nothing feels better than having that itch scratched."*

As you can see, there is nothing about the product or service or any selling at all. It's just the start of the story and it's designed to get the *interest* of the client so that they will read on to the next part of the email - the body copy.

### Body copy

The body copy is where you build the *desire* of the client to want what you have to offer. It's not as long or involved as a sales letter, it can be short and to the point - I have what you want, you need it, come to me to get it. But if you are telling a story, you may want to use more finesse. This isn't always necessary, but you can test it as you will be sending out hundreds, if not thousands, of emails in your business life once you understand how powerful this tactic is.

**Anyway, the body copy of the *"An itch you have to scratch"* email went like this:**

*Not a great example, but I had a new client In the salon the other day, Candy, and she was looking for a very specific hairstyle. You see, she was going to a work party and she was dressed as a 1920s flapper. And she wanted a 1920s hairstyle.*

*Specifically, finger waves.*

*Finger waves are waves moulded into the hair by, um, fingers. Giving a wavy pattern close to the head.*

*Candy started out on her quest to get exactly what she wanted.*

*Exactly what she envisaged in her head of the perfect hairstyle to achieve her look. Five salons later she walks into mine. Five salons said no, they couldn't do finger waves, but what about something else? Five salons, with say an average of five stylists per salon, that's 25 stylists who could not manage one of the iconic hairstyles of the 1920s.*

*25 stylists who would not be able to work as session stylists on fashion shoots. 25 stylists who are really letting down the hairdressing industry by not actually learning the craft of hairstyling.*

*25 stylists who lost a client.*

*But not my problem, because when Candy came in to enquire, I said yes, of course I can do finger waves.*

*And I proceeded to give Candy the look she wanted.*

*And that's down to finding someone who has experience, who has chosen hairdressing as a career, and cares about hair and the wants and needs of clients who come into the salon.*

*And that goes for the rest of my team too. All hand selected by me.*

*Just have a think about that for a minute.*

*And then, stop thinking and get down here to get your wants sorted out.*

*Speak soon.*

*Terry xx*

The body copy should contain at least one hyperlink - before the call to action - that the client feels compelled to click on, but only for entertainment purposes. In the above email, there was a link on *"the look she wanted",* which took the client to a photo of Candy, with her 1920s do, standing next to Terry, who was grinning like a loon.

If you 'train' your clients to click on links early on, it will pay out when it comes to your *Call To Action*, but more about that in a minute. Your links can be to a photo, a video or a page, but don't make them to another person's website or to Facebook, or to anywhere else that is going to distract the reader from continuing to read down to the Call To Action.

### Call To Action

In the example I've given, the Call To Action is: *"Stop thinking and get down here and get your wants sorted out."* This was set as a link to the salon's online booking page. As soon as the client clicked on it they were able to make an appointment straight away.

Your Call To Action can be your offer, but it needs to be strong enough to get the client to do something. *"Give us a call sometime,"* is a weak and ineffective Call To Action; it's telling the reader that you may or may not like to do this, it's up to you. *"Get your hair pain taken away here,"* is a stronger Call To Action if it is linked to a booking form. *"Call xxxxxxxxx number now to be one of 20 to receive a free treatment with your next service,"* is also a strong CTA. Whatever your offer is, make sure the client can do something with it whilst it is in front of them, when they are reading it.

### P.S.

There's always a P.S. in my emails. It's the coda or tail of an email that you can have fun with, and it will surprise and delight your reader. The P.S. works well if it is part of an ongoing story, quite separate from the body copy story you have just written about, and it's just a small snippet of an amusing or intriguing story that compels the reader to want to open the email tomorrow...

For example, one of the P.S. sequences I wrote was about Terry's quest to get fit for some mid-distance open water swims he was doing for charity. This is one from the sequence:

*"P.S. Remind me to tell you tomorrow about my friend Jarred who competed in the gruelling NZ Coast to Coast event without being able to swim. More brawn than brains. In the meantime, use your brains and get in here now."*

And I hope you've realised that the *"get in here now"* was a link to the online booking page again. The P.S. not only acts as a teaser to make people want to open the email tomorrow, but it also reinforces your Call To Action again.

You know you have written a good email when you get people to take up your offer, and also when you get a response, whether positive or negative. In fact, getting a negative response means that you are doing your job of polarising your list, so look forward to those ones. And remember, they are not a personal attack, just an emotional response to something you've said that they want you to fix for them.

**Here's one I really enjoyed writing and the (positive) response from a client:**

*Hi Steve,*

*Ever had one of those days?*

*My business partner, Kat, just has.*

*It started out at 2.30am when the little friend of her daughter, Heléna, cried out for her mummy. She was staying for a sleepover and got a little scared when she woke to find she wasn't in her own bed, as 7-year-olds do. So Kat had to cuddle her back to sleep. Then the party started again at 5.30am when two excited 7-year olds decided that sleep was for wussies and giggled their way around the house.*

*Sleep is overrated.*

*Little friend dispensed with at 10am, and it was off to the park to enjoy water fountains, go-karts, playground equipment and sunshine. Well, she does live in the Middle East and the balmy winter sun is very pleasant to be in at this time of year.*

*A few hours later and it was time to head home. Heléna complained that she was not feeling very well, but Kat put it down to too much sun, too much running about and not enough sleep. They got into the lift in the apartment building, pushed the button to the 16th floor and off they went.*

*By the 4th floor, Heléna was looking very pale, by the 7th floor the first gush of vomit came out all over the floor, by the 11th floor the second gush. Just in time for the doors to open and the other occupant of the lift (oh, I forgot to say someone else was in the lift with them) to get out. With her went some of the vomit - down the crack of the doors and into the lift shaft.*

*The kind lady offered to help but Kat had seen the vomit splatter on her black patent shoes and was mortified, so she said thanks but no thanks. Lift kept going up to the 16th floor, at which point Heléna was bundled out and taken to the apartment for a shower.*

*Kat rode back down with the vomit lift to the ground floor. Two security guards, two building managers and a cleaner later, the lift was sealed off and fumigated.*

*Kat got the next lift back up to the apartment, covered in vomit splatter, and commenced 'operation clean-up, soothing and put-to-bed'.*

*Yes, one of those days.*

*Sounds like she could do with a wine.*

*Or even a relaxing treatment in the salon, with a glass of wine.*

*Alas she can't, it's too far away, so she'll have to wait.*

*But you don't need to. You can get in right now. And you don't have to have had a day like this to benefit from the experience that a treatment in the salon gives you.*

*Now that's a relief.*

*Speak soon,*

*Terry xx*

*P.S. In fact, Kat has not just had one of those days, she's had one of those weeks: downloaded a movie on her phone without thinking about how she was connected to the internet - £200; driving out of a shopping mall with the hatchback of the car wide open, wondering why the view in the rear vision mirror was so clear; booking tickets for the cinema, getting to security and being told they were for tomorrow's movie, not today's. She could definitely use some pampering. So could you, so what are you waiting for?*

The response?

*"Brilliant email, Kat –I could almost smell it! It's like I'm sat in the bar listening to you. In my head the words have got a Kiwi accent to them!"*

*Steve Barnett*

*Hexagon IT*

---

Golden rule - write like you speak.

---

## Technical difficulties and formats

The problem with the fancy pants done-for-you templates with lots of photos in them is that not everyone is on the same system as you, and email providers vary in terms of what you can see when you send an email. You will, I am sure, have received emails from companies that a) take forever to download but, more importantly, b) are full of blank boxes with a question mark or other place holders where a picture is supposed to be but isn't because it's in the wrong format for whatever you are using.

If the prime desire for your email marketing is for your client to actually read your message, this type of formatting is worse than useless. They are also designed to 'tell' rather than 'sell', so it's a bit like browsing through a catalogue with a morning cup of coffee instead of reading a story that is selling with a clear Call To Action.

To get around this, I use simple HTML, indenting the first line of each paragraph, justifying the paragraph and using italics, bold and occasionally highlighting, with links to pictures, videos, web pages and sales forms.

Open rates and click through rates are often talked about, as if increasing them is the holy grail of email marketing. It's not, sales are. You might have an email that was opened by 50% of your readers and made you 9 sales, or an email that was opened by only 13% of your readers and made you 21 sales. And of course, the type of sales they were and the money in your pocket is going to determine the success of the emails you send, not the open or click through rates. And bear in mind that it can be very hard to determine whether any one email is the best email.

You have to factor in the length of time you have been emailing that person, what your offer is and if it is time-limited, as well as a whole host of other variables. Growth will be a cumulative effect. The key is to keep emailing. Which is why I call it relentless follow up.

### Deliverability

*"The war for your inbox"* is a good way to describe all the crap out there that is forcing its way through the ether towards your unsuspecting inbox. There are spammers galore who want to know if you worry about the length of your penis, or if you want to meet and marry a hot Ukrainian. This is why there are also filters and blockers to help keep your inbox spam-free, but these can inadvertently prevent your message from getting through too.

### Spam

Don't be tempted to buy lists. There are companies about that will sell you lists of names and addresses. Yes, that is where your spam comes from. Data companies buy lists and then sell those lists onto the unsuspecting, or the douchebags, or the just plain stupid. If you send emails to a cold list who haven't opted in to your offer, who haven't the slightest clue who you might be and who you haven't nurtured yourself, you are going to royally piss-off a lot of people, and maybe even fall foul of the many new 'rules' around emailing lists in a few different countries.

You want targeted prospects opting in to your emails so that you have a better chance of selling your product or service to a willing person. Contacting someone who doesn't fit your profile of your ideal client is a waste of your time and money. And they can be very vocal about your tactics, which is a ball ache at best and a right legal hassle at worst. Bottom line: Don't spam.

### Autoresponders and email systems

If you have a computerised salon reservation system, which contains your database of clients, your appointments and your sales information, you may also have an automated emailing system. For example, the system I used in the salon captured all the client data that was inputted once the client had come into the salon for the first time. Then we bought a bolt-on product from the software company that allowed us to automate our marketing and pulled the information from the database so we could send out emails to the entire client list, or to limited segmented parts of it. I used this system to send out daily emails to clients.

Most reservation systems will have something similar, but it may have been sold to you for sending out email vouchers, birthday wishes or messages that say, *"We haven't seen you in six months, is it something we said?"* These usually come complete with those cheesy templates and involve lots of formatting and faffing around.

This system works absolutely fine for all the clients you currently have, all of whom will have come into the salon and bought something - a service or product. But they don't have the capacity to collect client data from someone who has been directed to your webpage from a slick piece of offline or online advertising and filled in their details in exchange for an offer - your report or 'how to' video. These are potential clients who have raised their hand and said: *"I'm interested, but before I commit to you I want to at least know the colour of your eyes."*

On the other hand, autoresponder software hosts your database and then does toe-curlingly awesome things, such as segmenting your list so you can target specific interests. For instance, how to care for your hair when you are pregnant or breastfeeding, changing your hair colour or finding the right shampoo for your hair type, etc. Then you can automatically send information to each segment that the people within those segments are specifically interested in.

This way your clients will become more predisposed to buy from you. In the main, setting up a sequence of emails that the new prospect receives after they have hit your webpage and received your free offer is a great way to start a relationship and establish some trust with them BEFORE they have set foot in the salon or even picked up the phone. This is transformational selling at it's fucking finest.

Autoresponders come in all shapes and sizes, from free use (depending on your list size and how many emails you send), to monthly subscriptions for sophisticated ones that do everything bar fixing you a G&T. You will need to do your research to get the right one for you. If you grow quickly - and you will if you do the work - you may want to consider investing in a paid-for service, as moving an existing list over to a new autoresponder can be like a molar extraction - easy and painless to sign up for but aching and sore as fuck for weeks afterwards.

Some examples of autoresponders are Mailchimp, Aweber, Ontraport, Infusionsoft and Active Campaign.

## Why emails work

### *Front of consciousness*

You are there when they are ready to buy. This sounds a bit twee but not everyone is either looking for, or ready to buy your thing the moment you send an email. They may not even open your emails every day. But the day they do have the need you will be there, because you are emailing every day - or at least five days a week.

I hope you understand now why sending once-a-month emails is like pissing in the wind. You'll have to be pretty lucky for that email to coincide with your prospect wanting to buy what you are selling at that exact moment.

### Relationship building

The people on your list are getting to like you. The longer they stay on your list and look forward to your emails, the more they are going to trust you. If you are emailing like a friend emails them, they will like you. And it's fact that we buy from people we like.

### Personality marketing

You will be putting your personality into your email marketing. All of a sudden you will have taken a very commoditised service or product - haircuts or shampoo - and made it into a niche service. Nobody else can duplicate it, because it is unique to you. And because nobody else is selling 'you', you are not dragged into price wars and bargaining hell.

### You are selling not telling

Your emails are structured deliberately to get people to act on your offer. You are not just educating, giving away information or 'engaging' their interest. If you have put the emails together using the AIDA formula, it will be a true sales email.

---

## Real Life Examples

1. **At the tail end of 2013, I was facing a larger than expected tax bill (my fault for not harassing the accountant for information in a timely fashion), so with cash flow a bit tight due to the boiler blowing up and losing a staff member, I sent out an email campaign (of about 15 emails) to my existing clients.** The offer was to prebook all of their 2014 appointments. The proposition was that I was going to raise the prices on 1 Jan 2014, but if they prebooked all their

appointments for this year they would only pay 2013 prices. I also offered for their appointments to be concierge managed by the reception team, who would send out reminders and call them each month to check that everything was OK. These 15 emails generated £72,000 in sales.

2.  **When I first started email marketing, I was a bit unsure about what my offer would be.** So I did a soft launch to test the response (yes, I too was a doubter and a bit anxious about what other people would think - it happens to the best of us). Terry was undertaking an open water swim in the Thames and we wanted to raise money for The Little Princess Trust (the charity that makes real hair wigs for children who have lost their hair due to illness or genetic disorder). So I emailed the list over a period of three weeks, with the Call To Action being to donate to our purpose-built charity page. The campaign got a great reaction and we raised over £3,000 for the charity.

## Chapter 11. Summary

→ **Email marketing, when done the QBofE way, is one of the best ways to build a relationship with a client and make sales.**

→ **Daily emails are not spam, they need to be entertaining and reflect your personality.** They are a great way to polarise your list and build a raving, loyal fan base.

→ **Everyone can write a daily email using the structure set out in this chapter.** Write like you speak.

→ **Emails work because you are front-of-consciousness when the client is ready to buy.** When you put your personality into the emails, clients associate your service or product with you, which takes you from a commoditised product to a niche product. Nobody else can replicate you.

### Take Action

Start emailing your list. Set up an autoresponder and begin. Tell them that you are going to send them a regular, if not daily, email that they will enjoy. But also tell them that they can unsubscribe at any time.

# CHAPTER TWELVE

# OTHER SOURCES OF TACTICS – THE ENDLESS LIST

The list of tactics for you to get your message in front of your ideal client is infinite and only limited by your imagination. I am not going to go into these following tactics in great detail, and you can probably think of plenty of others, but here are the main ones:

## Where Else Do Your Clients Hang Out?

### Yellow pages ads

Yes, people still receive and read the printed Yellow Pages, particularly the older demographic. If this is your niche then test it. Just make sure your ad follows the AIDA principle.

### Blogs

Blogs are useful in that you can drive traffic from them to your webpage or landing page opt-ins. If you are writing daily emails, you have already created content for your blog. Simple.

### TV

Regional TV channels offer advertising per 30 seconds of advert. This may be something to consider if you are targeting a specific tight geographical niche, but you will have to weigh up the cost with the ROI. In New Zealand, there is a butcher who is a national icon. Peter Leitch, aka *The Mad Butcher*, has been in business since 1971, but I specifically remember his personality-filled adverts on TV during the 1980s. At that time I think he had two or three retail butcher locations. When I was back in New

Zealand in 2015, I was surprised to see that *The Mad Butcher* adverts were still on TV.

Leitch now has 40 outlets throughout NZ and does some pretty cool things for community fundraising. TV advertising worked for him for a number of reasons: he started with local TV advertising, he had a good product, he put his full personality into his marketing (what you saw on TV was what he was like in the shop), he bundled his products, he wasn't cheap but he showed his value and he had a strong Call To Action. And because it worked he continued to do it.

Alternatively, follow the example of a fellow Elite marketing mastermind group member and create your own online TV channel. Paul Mort's business *'Unstoppable Bastards'*, targets married businessmen who want to do better in business, but also want to get in shape, have more power, become a bad-ass dad and be a great husband with an unbreakable mindset. This is a big task if my husband is anything to go by, but Paul is funny and smart and has a fantastic Geordie accent. He created his own TV channel to 'show' rather than 'tell' what it takes for him to be the leading expert in this tightly-defined niche. Of course, the channel is a tactic to get leads to a landing page where they see a one hour documentary (sales pitch) and apply for a personal interview with Paul to see if they are the right fit for him. Genius. (If you are interested, he's at: www.iampaulmort.com.)

### Local radio

Radio advertising is a cost-effective way to get your message out to many people, particularly in smaller communities. There is still a demographic that listens to daytime radio and their many adverts, my mum being one of them which is how she found her hairdresser in a new town. Create your ad with AIDA principles in mind and have a unique code with your Call To Action so that you can measure the response.

## Instagram

Instagram is owned by Facebook, and the ads are built through their Power Editor API. In other words, you will need a business Facebook page to advertise on Instagram, although they are starting to roll out their own ad creation area. So if you decide to use this, you will need to incorporate the same targeting principles as with Facebook. Instagram has a more 'highbrow creative' philosophy than Facebook when it comes to what ads it will let you have, which may align quite nicely with high-end salons. The thing in its favour is that it's relatively new and not many advertisers are on it yet. It's another bright shiny thing and there's no harm in testing it along with the other tactics in your arsenal, as long as your strategy is sound.

## Pinterest

This is a place for your creative outlet and it's a great platform to have your 'photo album'. But don't spend too much time on that side of it. Pinterest has a promoted pin type of advert, much like Facebook's sponsored post, but it is very restrictive in what you can advertise so bear that in mind.

## Twitter

I've yet to foray into Twitter ads, mostly because I had major problems with my account being regularly hacked a few years ago, so I gave it the shove. But for research purposes I've found that they allow you to advertise with clicks through to your webpage. With a limit of 140 characters you will need to be slick with your headline and create instant attention. If your prospects are likely to be on Twitter, test it.

This may be a geographical or even a cultural thing, but where I am currently living in the Middle East, Twitter is the king of social media. All events are advertised through Twitter as opposed to websites (which are fucking dire, I can tell you). Maybe this has something to do with the Bedouin 'word-of-mouth' way of communicating. Whatever. If that's your market, then it would be silly not to test it.

## PR

You can pay for a PR company to do PR for you, but you will need to be very sure about what it is you are wanting them to do in terms of getting clients in the door, and in my experience this type of PR is usually in the form of non-measurable 'brand awareness' and 'social engagement', rather than in the more effective and useful direct response marketing. But you can effectively PR yourself, which is a bonus as it is free. The best book I have read about how to successfully PR your product or service is *'Build a Business From Your Kitchen Table'*, written by *notonthehighstreet.com* founders Sophie Cornish and Holly Tucker.

## App

Here I'm talking about having your own app where you can send traffic for urgent needs and appointments. Apps and technology are so sophisticated now that you can target people with a push message from your app as they walk past your salon, enticing them in. For existing clients, that is a great way to be front of their mind. But for new prospects be wary of the quality. A notification selling heavily discounted services for a space you haven't filled will attract price-buyers and all the shit that comes with them, making you 'that type of salon'.

## Printed Newsletters

I have talked a little about printed newsletters in Chapter eight as part of continuity and keeping your clients loyal. So I mention this here to say that a regular monthly printed newsletter is something that you can give away free to get a new client opt-in, and it's a useful tool to keep clients coming back to you. If you use a free printed newsletter as part of your lead generation, you will have to take note that it is a long game. Getting business from this method is hard to measure but the indicators are similar to email marketing, a printed newsletter is a constant reminder to your lead that you exist.

Given that there are so many options, what is going to work for you? I can't tell you, just pick one and start. Alternatively, pick one that you might have already started, check the numbers and tweak it to make it better. I can't guarantee the results you will get but I can guarantee that if you don't do any traffic generation, you won't get any clients.

> Of course, the holy grail of direct response marketing is to use both online and offline marketing in a sequence or a system.

By this I mean having a comprehensive funnel where your leads are put into a sequence and receive as many 'touches' from you as possible, relentlessly until they die, buy, or ask you to fuck off. It may look something like: Lead is 'interrupted' by a Facebook ad on his newsfeed and clicks the link, which takes him to your landing page with a video and compelling sales copy that asks him to 'opt-in' to receive a free PDF report, which can also be posted out to a physical address. The lead is then put into a sequence of emails that provides more info about your thing and why it would solve his problem. This builds a relationship.

At the end of the sequence, the lead is asked to buy your product or service and is placed on a daily email list, in order to be followed up relentlessly. At the same time the lead receives a postcard, some lumpy mail and a sales letter asking him to buy your offer. This is a very simple system and anyone can do it. Once you get into it, the extra steps you can take are immense and your system can get very sophisticated. (It can also be automated so you don't have to worry about keeping track of every stage.) But once you get into it, the whole thing can get very exciting. And it's also very profitable.

## Chapter 12. Summary

→ **There are many other platforms to use to get your message to clients.**

→ **Your choice of medium is only limited by your imagination.** In the beginning, stick to the 80/20 Principle and use the platform that is likely to give you the best ROI for your target audience.

→ **There is no guarantee that any platform will work for you;** you will just have to test it. But I can guarantee that if you don't do anything at all, you won't generate any leads.

→ **Combine offline marketing with online marketing for the ultimate marketing system.**

### Take Action

Just like with Chapter 10, pick a medium from this list and start advertising on it.

*Part Three*

# YOUR
# MESSAGE

# CHAPTER THIRTEEN
## SELLING - THE DIRTY WORD

I know you know how to sell. It's part of your remit. And your suppliers all have training programmes and incentives in place to sell more of their products. So you're creaming it with the add-on sales and the upsells in the salon, right? So why are you getting so much resistance from your staff to sell to their clients? If you are hearing, *"I don't like the hard sell, and my clients don't either,"* they are missing the whole point of selling. No one likes to be forced to buy something, and it makes you look desperate and unprofessional at the same time.

When you mention the word 'selling' it conjures up images of greasy used-car salesmen or young, pushy real estate agents hungry for commission and caring little about you or your needs. To them anyone is a client and it is a matter of just going through numbers of people before the sale is in the bag. They are perceived as pushing you into buying something that you don't need or want. Well, selling is not a bad thing and if done properly can be one of the most pleasant experiences in the world.

> More like being softly and deftly seduced and wanting to open your wallet to whatever the offer is.

Warning - the art of persuasion and selling is pretty powerful once you know it and how people respond, so I am talking about *ethical* selling. Something I will only engage in. I wouldn't work with an 'alternative healing' provider for example, no matter how much someone wanted to buy from them. That's the thing. The majority of the time clients buy on 'want', not 'need'. Do I need the latest iPhone release when my Nokia 6010 still works as a telephone? No, but I want it, just because I love Apple products and would marry one if I could. Do I need a new hair colour? Not really, I could go grey slowly as nature and my genetics has designed and save myself some hours in the chair. Do I need that beautiful, shiny organically-farmed apple presented in a handmade wooden box with gold tissue paper that costs £150, when I could pick one off the tree in the garden, a bit misshapen but edible, for free? (Well, at the time of writing this I live in the Middle Eastern desert and there are no apple trees, just sand, so that's not really a good example. I could definitely get the former golden apple though).

But you get the picture.

People buy on what they want, not what they need. So you can tailor the way you sell your products and services to their desires and aspirations. And whilst no one likes a hard sell, don't use this as an excuse not to do it at all. You are doing your client and yourself a disservice if you are not asking for the sale. You are in business to make money, pure and simple. And if you have an ethical, morally sound and legal business, you know your client will benefit from what you are selling them. There is an exchange of value both ways: you're selling them something they want which makes them feel good, and you're making money and have a business that is successful and lasts longer.

So, in order to understand how to sell in a soft and seductive way, we need to understand how we as humans are influenced.

## The Six Triggers Of Influence

Robert Cialdini showed fairly conclusively back in the 1970s that there are six very powerful triggers to persuasion buried deep in the brain - and these are indeed down to our neurology not social conditioning, because they are not dependent on race or culture. What influences a male Estonian will influence a female Egyptian.

**Cialdinis's triggers are:**

1. **Reciprocity:** If you do something for me, I feel obliged to do something for you in return. Go back to the stand in the supermarket where they are handing out free cubes of cheese on a toothpick. Once you accept that free, 1cm cubed piece of solid, fermented milk, you're more compelled to buy the block. That free sample of shampoo in a gift bag? You're more likely to want to rebook an appointment.

2. **Authority:** We tend to obey authority figures. Hot firemen in uniform; check. Police; check. Doctors; check. Salon owners; ummmmm. Salon owners who are the expert in their niche and have got the fucking book to prove it; check. If you have authority you are more likely to be obeyed and get compliance from your clients.

3. **Scarcity:** We want what we can't have. And I don't mean you are not allowed it. But you want and there aren't enough to go around. There are plenty of examples here of queues around the block for the next limited edition Apple product, paying a fortune for a special number plate, a painting, a watch. I've seen grown woman fighting with each other over a place for their child in a space-limited swimming squad. Sad but true. *"I only have 10 bottles of this product at this special price, once they've gone they're gone, and I don't know if this offer will be available again."* Disney use this tactic repeatedly in their 'Offers from the Vault.' They release classic videos for a limited period and then put them back in the 'Vault', so they are unavailable to purchase, sometimes for years.

4. **Consistency and Commitment:** We tend to feel obliged to act in the way we have said we're going to act. This is particularly relevant when you write things down, such as goals. Written goals are more likely to be acted upon. When we tell those goals to trusted friends and family we are also likely to achieve them so we look consistent.

5. **Liking:** We tend to be more easily influenced by people we like, than by people we don't. That's why it is so important to put yourself and your personality into your marketing. Your client is not buying from your brand or your business, they are buying from you. If you are attracting your ideal client and repelling the client from hell, you will be pulling in people who are predisposed to like you.

6. **Social Proof:** We tend to follow the crowd, and a great example of this is the power of Testimonials. If your clients are raving about you to their friends, and the results show, you are more likely to see their friends in your door because of social proof.

When you put these influencers into a sales piece, or sales pitch, you are going to hit the sweet spot with your prospect. And you will undoubtedly also hit it with your current clients, in fact you will need to do even less work towards selling to your raving fans as they will have already experienced you and your service and the liking, social proof and authority will have already been established.

When selling a product or service to a client, ensure you are selling the benefits not the features. *"The bottle has a pump nozzle,"* is a feature. *"The pump nozzle on the bottle measures the exact amount of product you need each time; there is no waste, you don't get a greasy build-up in your hair/on your face, and the product will last longer,"* is a rather long sentence but is showing the client the benefits, and a reason to buy.

## Your Sales Piece Message

### The AIDA principle

I touched on the AIDA (Attention, Interest, Desire, Action) principle in *Chapter 9 - Online Advertsing* and *Chapter 11 - Email Marketing*, but you should be using the AIDA principle in all forms of your message. From your website, to your emails, to your adverts, to your free reports. Think of the adverts that catch your attention, and then make you pause longer than the average 8 seconds it takes most people to skip past one. What is it about the ad that attracted you? What made you want to read on? What made you want to take action?

Most advertising you will see speaks not to the client but to the jumped-up ego of the company and their brand. In fact, 99% of big company brand advertising is a waste of time and money for the small business owner, and you should never do it. But back to the AIDA principle. This works because it takes the prospect on a structured path from getting their Attention in a very busy environment (whether it be an online ad, or a letter in the post), to creating Interest by showing them they have a problem. Sometimes a problem that they didn't even know was a problem until you show them something tangible.

Then you create Desire by agitating that problem and then telling them you have a solution to their problem, using persuasion to show that your solution is the bespoke solution. Then you lead them to exactly how they can get hold of this solution from you. Throughout this process you tell them, tell them that you've told them, and then tell them again.

## Attention

I'm not a copywriter, not even close, but over time I have used a lot of this info to help write sales pages, headlines, ads and copy. Once you have the guidelines in place, writing something decent, readable and, most of all, compelling won't be too hard, but it will take practice, practice, practice, and a healthy dose of testing and measuring to get it right. Or you could outsource your copywriting and get a copywriter that knows how to write for DRM. Be warned, not all are created equal and some haven't a clue about how to write for DRM.

I made an expensive mistake with the first copywriter I hired through a friend, before I knew what I was doing. And it wasn't that he was more interested in my boob size than my font size, he just didn't have a clue. It wasn't that he wasn't experienced in copywriting, just that his experience was in (apart from tit ogling) big corporate businesses that talk about themselves and what they can do for you. Not about your clients' problems and how you have the solution to alleviating their pain. I should have taken the warning at the first meeting when my boobs were the most fascinating thing in the room, but I ended up with copy I had to pay for that was, for all intents and purposes, worthless. If you find the right copywriter hang on to them and pay them well, the return on investment will be worth it.

**In the meantime, if you want to attempt it yourself here are some rules for writing to get your prospects dribbling and quivering for more:**

For eye-catching headlines, kickers, opening paragraphs and even PPC or Facebook ads, there's a very simple formula you can use:

1. Call out to readers feeling the *pain* you are going to ease.

2. Promise a *solution* or a cure to reverse the damage.

3. Promise an additional *big benefit* above and beyond merely easing the pain.

**For example:**

1. Suffering from embarrassing frizz?

2. The QBofE Treatment Plan will smooth your hair back to baby-softness in just 6 weeks...

3. And guarantee you that hot date with that guy you fancy the pants off.

OK maybe a bit OTT with some of the claims there, but you get the picture. The best headlines have their own rhythm, and you will know that when you read it out loud and see it. It takes practice to write but you will figure out the good ones pretty quickly, as you will see a massive bump in response when it happens.

## Interest

What do your clients really want?

Instead of faff-arsing about doing things that you think your clients might like, ask them what they really want. And I'm not talking about feedback. Feedback can be as much use as tits on a bull. It's a person's opinion based on their own emotional reactions. Opinions are like arseholes, everyone has one, but no one wants one waved in their face (well some people do but that's another book altogether).

No, I'm talking about what challenges your clients have and what you can do to solve them. At the back of my book *'101 Naked Confessions of a Gay Hairdresser',* the Call To Action asks the reader to write down the three goals they have for their hair and the challenges that prevent them from achieving them. The response you get from this question is usually so detailed that you will have no trouble coming up with a solution (a service or a product) that will meet the needs of the client and they will buy it in spades. But also, you can come up with the information you need to create interest. You know what their problems are because they have told you, but when you write it up it will sound to them like you have really got inside their head and understand them completely.

**Here's an example:**

*What is your goal for your hair in the next six months?*

To get it healthy and shiny, so it looks like I have just been to the salon and is easy to care for.

*What are the top three challenges that are preventing you from reaching that goal?*

1.  Not having time to use treatments regularly.
2.  Not knowing how to use products and tools properly. Hard to get to the bits at the back.
3.  Don't know what suits me.

If you ignore the time and suitability challenge for a moment, there is a great opportunity with creating a service for number two.

## Real Life Example

One of the services we created after we read this was a *'Knowledge Session'.* I know a few salons do this but at the time I didn't, so we thought we were pretty cool. We allowed clients an appointment to come into the salon with all the products and tools they had at home and we would show them how to use them properly and how to do their hair in a couple of different styles that were easy for them to achieve. It was fun for the clients as they were getting personalised time and would benefit from the information given. The stylist enjoyed being able to show off their knowledge, and 8 times out of 10 we could recommend fewer and better products (our own), which the clients would purchase. The added bonus was this little service started to create client loyalty and repeat business as they used our products and our styling techniques to achieve that 'salon look' at home.

The questions can be used in any business or any aspect of your life. It's that powerful. You can ask yourself the same question for your business. In fact, I have done exactly that in the Appendix of this book. You can think about it now and fill it in for me. I promise I will respond to you.

## Desire

When you are selling your products or services there are ethical ways to hook the client into your story so that they feel more compelled to buy from you, or to want to find out more about your offer. These tricks are well-known but human nature being what it is, we think of ourselves as free-willed, that we are clever enough and witted enough to make logical and rational decisions given the information. We are far from being amoebic-like in our actions, where stimulus results in response, but we are not really that far removed. There are emotional hot buttons and triggers that influence the way we think and psychologists, along with marketers, have studied human behaviour for centuries and the same things come up time and time again. You can use these elements to show your prospect what you are promising to provide to take away the pain from their suffering.

### Exclusivity

Do you have a product that is exclusive to you? Have you thought about 'white-labelling' a product or two? This involves negotiating with a supplier to have a generic product, e.g., styling spray or nail strengthener labelled with your own brand. It's not difficult to do, and some suppliers don't require huge batch runs.

In fact, we had a supplier who would give us the unlabelled product as we needed it, and we stuck our own labels on in the back room! That product was exclusive to our salon - you couldn't get it anywhere else. You can even be exclusive with your services in the most commoditised market. You can get a haircut anywhere but you can't get the (insert your name here) signature cut anywhere else.

### Scarcity

Provide limited access to yourself and your service, or a limited number of the product you have to offer. Be genuine with this though, if you only have 50 products to sell for this offer, don't suddenly come up with 10 or 20 more. Limiting the amount of clients you see, or the time you spend on the floor also creates scarcity.

But before you get all het-up and say more clients make you more money, rethink the proposition. If you could have three clients per day maximum, and provide a service that they could have nowhere else, something that required your full and exclusive attention, and they got the VVVVIP treatment with the star and their name on the door, and you charged 10x the normal amount for it, that would be worth it, no?

### Take away selling

I'm not for everyone. Back to Cialdini and people wanting what they can't have: if you tell someone you're not for them, they will want you more. If you tell someone you're probably not the best fit for them, they will say, *"Why not?"* If you tell someone your waiting list is closed, they will bug you until you find a space for them.

> The hardest thing you have to do to get a client through your door is establish trust.

If you are giving your prospect a 'get out clause' even before they are in, it gives them back the power of making the decision to buy from you. It turns the sale on its head, from you selling to them, to them wanting to buy only from you.

### Early Bird and Early Deadline

This is loosely related to scarcity, but if you are looking for a cash-flow fix, hurry the sale along with an early bird price that your client can take advantage of and feel like they have made a saving. *"Buy before the 17th of May, when the price will go up another 200 dollars."*

### Add premiums and bonuses

*"If you buy now you will also receive another service or product worth x for free. But only as part of this offer."*

### A reason to believe

When creating desire, you also need a reason to believe. The client needs to believe that you and only you can cure their pain, and that your solution will fix their problem.

**You can do this in a number of ways, but there are a couple of very simple ones that you should always try to incorporate:**

1.  **Guarantee**

    A cast iron guarantee. One that is specific, measurable and has a high perceived value, so it puts the onus on you to deliver what you promise, and any reluctant prospect has a trust safety net. Eliminating the risk is what your guarantee needs to do. Make it bold and relevant and, if you are called out on it, make sure you honour it, no question. If you offer a 100% money back guarantee, refund in full. *"If you don't see a noticeable difference with softer hair in six weeks, then I will refund you in full."*

2.  **Testimonials**

    You will probably have a load of these already as people are always being asked for reviews on third-party sites - Facebook, Twitter, Yelp, Yell.com, whatever your country supports in terms of a social proof platform. The 'sell' that these platforms tell you is that people will see their friend's recommendations and want to buy from you as well. It's a tenuous link to social proof, but it is hard to measure.

    The better way is to have a robust referral system, but testimonials can be used in your sales pieces so you can get a 'real life' point of view across. If you can get a video testimonial from a client, even better. Try to use testimonials specific to the product or service you are selling. If you can't get a video, include the photo and location of the client giving it to you. This increases credibility.

## Action

Finally, you must always have a Call To Action (CTA) at the end of your sales piece. The CTA must be an absolutely crystal clear method of response. It must be strong, and so simple a toddler could do it. You should only have one call to action, e.g., if you want someone to book an appointment, *that* is the CTA, and you should tell them exactly how to do it. If there is only one way, by phone for example, tell them the number to call and the time to call, and who to ask for.

**If you have a number of ways to book an appointment then you can list them like so:**

*"To take advantage of this offer you need to book an appointment with me by 6pm, 10th of March. You can make a booking in three easy ways:*

1. *Call the salon on xxxxx between x and x Monday to Sunday and speak to Y and she will confirm your appointment straight away.*

2. *Email the salon at salon@salon.com and put 'Fantastic Offer' in the subject line and tell us the date you want and we will book for you straight away.*

3. *Book online at www.salon.com on our online reservation system. Click on 'Book now' and follow the simple steps. Use the code 'FanOff' in the offer box. You will get a confirmation straight away."*

Be specific and accurate and give them the CTA again in the P.S. Tell them, tell them you've told them, and tell them again.

Finally, again, the golden rule is, *'write like you speak'.* Change all the instances of 'we' and 'us' to 'you' and 'I'. Clients don't care about your company and your thing and how 'professional' you sound, they want to be at the centre of your marketing and get a solution to their problem. That may sound selfish, but I guarantee that's exactly what you look for when you are buying from someone.

### And on a final, final note:

Don't be desperate. If you are throwing yourself on the mercy of your clients and doing everything you can think of to get the sale, your clients will sense your desperation in all its unattractive glory and it will create the 'limp dick syndrome'. They'll stop buying from you.

Discounts can show desperation and it sets you up in the client's mind that once you give discounts, they will always get discounts. I know that my ex-business partner was giving his long-term clients discounts every time they came to the salon. So much so, they were paying the same prices as they were seven years before, despite the fact that costs had gone up in the salon.

They are your clients not your friends, you are not running a charity. Don't be surprised when they don't necessarily complain, but try and make you feel guilty 'as a friend' about the cost of your service in one breath, whilst telling you about their awesome holiday to the Antipodes, and the purchase of a new phone in the next. If you are doing this, stop now. You are stealing from yourself and decreasing your own value.

If you show you can take or leave your clients business, but your rules are that your prices are not negotiable, you are back to positioning yourself as the best, the expert and the one that they will find the money to absolutely have.

## Advanced Bonus: Why Your Message Might Differ

If you are selling exclusively to women, or exclusively to men, you will want to tailor your message to suit each taste and psychological pull. Selling to most men, and the words you use, is very different from selling to most women. I say most because some women are more male brained than others and will not respond to some female-centric messages, and vice versa. But the 80/20 Principle applies here, so that's what I am going to go with. One of the best books I have read on this subject is 'Inside Her Pretty Little Head' by Jane Cunningham and Philippa Roberts. And it is from here that I will share some insights about the differences between selling to men and woman. Traditionally, marketing and advertising is written by and targets men. However, given that women in the USA, for example, account for 80% of all purchase decisions, the way it is written should be targeting them.

Perhaps the easiest and quickest way to show the differences is in the table on the next page.

When you are considering your message to clients and prospects, bear these in mind.

| Male | Female |
| --- | --- |
| Focus on Achievement.<br><br>Respond to: Status symbols, one-upmanship, politics and game-playing. | Naturally Altruistic, Nurturing and 'Others'-focused.<br><br>Respond to: ethical brand positioning, community-based promotion, altruistic values, giving back, fair trade, small business rather than large corporates. |
| Interest in Things Rather Than People.<br><br>Respond to: Function and form, darker, colder colours. | Attend to or are Naturally Interested in Aesthetics, Beauty Fads and Fashions.<br><br>Respond to: buying a piece of an aesthetically-enhanced world, making functional products and services pleasurable, bright and soft colours with human and natural motifs, beautiful packaging, focus on detail and close-ups. |
| Survival Through Self-Interest, Hierarchy, Power and Competition.<br><br>Respond to: Promise of sexual, work, and social success. | Relationship-Driven in Order to Survive.<br><br>Respond to: Networks or groups, belonging to a group or club, conversation, being 'in-the-know', the sub-text of a conversation. |
| Hard Wired to Systemise.<br><br>Respond to: Simple information with simple choices. | Take Care with Detail, Plan Ahead.<br><br>Respond to: Proactive services, attention to detail, a lot of information covering all risks and outcomes. |

For a much more in depth and fascinating explanation on how to market specifically to women, I can't recommend *'Inside Her Pretty Little Head'* enough.

## Chapter 13. Summary

→ **Selling is not a dirty word, and if it's done correctly it can be a pleasant, seductive experience for the buyer.**

→ **Clients buy what they 'want', not necessarily what they 'need', and they generally buy when they have a problem that they want solved.**

→ **Cialdini's Principles of Influence** – Reciprocity, Authority, Scarcity, Consistency, Liking and Social Proof can be used to tailor your message and persuade your prospect to buy from you.

→ **Your sales message should always follow the AIDA principle** – Attention, Interest, Desire, Action.

→ **Your sales message may differ depending on whether you are targeting men or women based on their tastes and psychological make-up.**

### Take Action

Read this chapter again to get to grips with all the elements of writing your message. Then incorporate these ideas into your sales pieces.

# *Part Four*
# YOUR
# MOTIVATION

# CHAPTER FOURTEEN
# JFDI - JUST FUCKING DO IT

The strategy and tactics I have talked about in this book are ways to grow your salon fast. This shit works, I know it does, not just in my previous salon, but I have seen it work in other businesses too. But it only works if you implement it. You might say *"Oh QBofE all that you have said is complete commonsense and it sounds a bit simple,"* well it is, but unless you are going to get stuck in and put it into practice, do the work and get your hands dirty, all you've done is read a book. And you'll still have the same business you started with when you picked this book up.

I can guarantee the people who use the strategies and tips in this book in their marketing, will not just see an increase in growth, but over time see an exponential increase in growth. It isn't easy, I admit, it is a lot of work, but there are ways to make implementing it a little easier, which I will share with you, but first a digression. I want to tell you a story about Just Fucking Doing It. The time in a previous life when I worked in Mental Health and I confronted a drug-dealing gang member...

Let's call him Danny, as that was his name.

He was well-known in the community as a bit of a bad egg.

I can't remember if it was him or his brother that killed someone with a sabre, but that pretty much sums up the status of this outstanding citizen. No respect for others.

Well the police didn't want a bar of them and I am sure that every time a call came in mentioning this particular family the shortest straw would've been the only way to deal with it.

I needed to stop him supplying drugs to my clients who were vulnerable and unpredictable if taking them. So the only way to do it was to get the police to issue a trespass notice on Danny.

So off I duly trotted to the local police station and asked to file a trespass notice.

The bloke at the counter gave me a notice to fill in, which I did and then handed it back.

*"Oh no,"* he says. *"We don't serve trespass notices on people any more, you will have to do it yourself."*

Whhaaaat?

*"Too scared? Too Busy?"*

*"No, it's just not our policy to do this any more."*

Too young and naïve to argue, I just thought, *"OK, I'll do it myself."*

Off I drive to Danny's house. Not hard to find.

I knock on the door.

*"This is for you,"* I say handing him the notice. *"Stop coming around to our houses and selling our guys drugs or I will call the Police."*

*"I'm not."*

*"Yes you are and if you do it again you will be in trouble."*

Ohhh - God, I'm tough.

I flounce off down the drive feeling pretty smug with myself. Scoffing at the police for not doing a simple job like that.

What did Danny do?

He did what all thug-like criminals do when they are confronted.

He rang his mummy.

How do I know?

His mum rang me and gave me a good telling off – How dare I harass her little boy, he's a good boy, etc.

By the end of that phone call I was shaking.

With laughter.

Two things I love about this story, (and it's completely true by the way. In fact, I was more in trouble with my husband when I got home and told him what I did. He thought I'd acted a bit recklessly, as we lived in a small town and, if they wanted, the family could have found where we lived and done a lot more than a shitty phone call) but back to the two things. I needed a solution to my problem and no one else was going to help so I just got out there and did it. I had no fear.

Afterwards, when I considered my husband's point of view, he probably had a fair point. But I tested it and got the results I needed. I could have sat there and considered all the options carefully and then given it up as a bad idea, but Danny would have still been bothering my clients and making them more ill with his drugs. But I took action and *Just Fucking Did It*, and although it turned out OK, I would have also been prepared to work through the consequences if it hadn't.

The second thing is that no matter what you do, there will always be someone out there that has some form of criticism. Unless these people are more successful than you, it's safe to ignore them. Or laugh at them, like I did with Danny's mum. She wasn't the slightest bit correct. Her son wasn't a good boy. Far from it. But If I had been worried about what she thought I wouldn't have taken action.

## You Want Me To Do What?

My point here is that if you want to grow your salon fast, you have to take action and implement the marketing ideas I have given you. The frustrating thing is that a lot of you won't and you will end up with the same business, if not worse, years from now, saying, *"I'm gonna,"* and then never actually *doing.*

The good thing is, there will be some of you that do take my advice and your business will prosper because of it. I guarantee that. It can be daunting to put it all together, or to know where to start. I know, I've been there. The trick is to just start and the rest will start to flow.

**What is it that holds you back from doing all of this?**

My guess is it not the time it takes, you can make time in your day or week easily by reorganising your priorities. It's probably not that you don't know what you are doing, there is plenty of material out there to help you, not least this book. You may not know where exactly to start, but again that's what this book is for. My guess, and a pretty educated one, is that the one thing that is holding you back is fear. Fear of being different from everyone else in the industry and being scorned for it. Fear of raising your head above the parapet and not being in the 'me too' pit. Fear, not of not knowing, but of not being perfect, or of failing. Yeah - it's that one in particular that we have an irrational fear of. Failing. It's a learnt response from our parents, friends and society and is a 'limiting belief'.

Really, what harm is embarrassment? What is the worst that can happen?

If you are marketing in the way I have shown you, some things will fail. But because you are testing things, measuring them, tweaking them and re-measuring, you will move on very quickly from failures and your successes will outweigh them. But the sheer fact that you are getting out of bed each day and you own a business, is setting you up for failures. If you didn't have a business and lay in bed watching TV each day, you wouldn't fail at all. The thing about being a failure in other people's eyes is that their opinion doesn't matter. It really doesn't. Not unless they are more successful than you in business. And then ask them how they do it.

You will have to grow a thick skin to fend off the helpful criticism from friends and family who think they are doing you a favour. And even your so-called competitors. But go with what has been tested and proven to work, even if it seems counterintuitive.

It works for a reason. And when your business is growing and you are doing well, that thick skin will also come in handy when you face jealousy and barbs about not deserving your success and wealth from those same friends and family. Even if you have had to work at it. And here's the trick: You do have to work at it. That's where most of you will fall down. This is work. You have to work hard and put the effort in to implement all this. Results will often not come straight away, but once the foundations are in place and you use more tactics, the growth will be exponential and you may just suffer from what a friend calls *"An embarrassment of income."* Not a bad place to be, and if you are looking for personal sovereignty and freedom, the *only* place to be.

---

## So you need to get started and JFDI - Just Fucking Do It.

---

When you look at all that you need to do, it does get overwhelming. I am constantly overwhelmed with the amount of work that needs to be done sometimes. But here's the trick: Pick somewhere and start. A great example is this book. I knew I wanted to write something for salon owners that has never been written before, and I knew I wanted the information in it to be of such quality that it can be used as a useful tool, not an ego-massaging coffee table bit of fluff. But initially the task was huge. There was so much information to give, where to start?

So I just picked a random point and started putting words down. Then gradually, the structure of the book started to come. I started listing the themes I wanted to cover and made bullet points for each theme, then I wrote a more detailed description for each bullet point and then just fleshed it out and filled in the gaps. As I was doing that I had more clarity about how it would work and changed the structure slightly, but, all of a sudden, there were 20,000 words staring at me, and then 20,000 more.

Don't let the thought of all this marketing overwhelm you, because that's when you will stop and do nothing. Break it down into bite-size chunks. It helps to prioritise your chunks too and pick the single most important task, the most useful thing that you can do most effectively right now and start. Once you start it will get easier, and once results come in you will be like a crack addict with a reliable supplier.

Make life easier for yourself and you will achieve more because you enjoy it more. There is a lot of information in this book, and I know it is daunting. I have been there. But I guarantee the overwhelm is tempered with a spot of relief. Relief that there is a way to grow your salon, there is a process to it, the strategies work, there are tactics to test and you will get results. The thing now is to have a plan. A plan to get you started and being able to do it.

The problem with most salon owners like yourself is that you are so involved in the day-to-day running of the salon, it is hard to fit anything 'extra' in without feeling like you are losing sleep, or losing control. By the end of a busy day on the floor you have dealt with late staff, sick staff, reconciled the till that someone else fucked up, spent time with your own clients, overseen a trainee's model, dealt with complaints from your staff's clients, fielded phone calls from suppliers, written up notes, planned a staff training session, had a cold cup of coffee and half a bite of a sandwich, watched a receptionist turn prospective clients away, dealt with more clients, noted that a washer needs replacing in the basin tap, changed the toilet roll, had another mouthful of cold coffee, talked, talked some more, helped the team clean up, locked up and gone home to crawl into bed, only to start the whole process again tomorrow.

And you want me to do *what*, Kat? You want me to find time to do some marketing? Are you out of your Queen Bitch of Everything mind?

The answer to that, of course, is *yes*.

You see, you can do this, it just involves some very basic changes to the way you are doing things now. Yes, that profane 'C' word that no one wants to say. Change. You might feel comfortable running around like a blue-arsed fly all day being 'busy'. But how much of what you are actually busy doing is productive and making you more money? Either bringing future business into the salon or making more money from existing business. Let's play my favourite game again.

**Would you rather:**

Be doing what you are doing every day until you retire and hopefully sell the business for a reasonable sum, but not have any energy to do anything because you are worn to the bone?

*or*

Would you rather have time for yourself now, with a business that runs well without you there 100% of the time, that you can sell for a considerable sum and then retire with energy to burn?

**It's not a dream. But you have to take the necessary steps now. And it is no simpler than doing the following three things:**

1. Outsource
2. Delegate
3. Automate

## Outsource

You can outsource a lot of things in the running of a business and also with the marketing of a business. The key is to find people or suppliers you can trust to do the job, which may require some oversight from you at the beginning until you are confident they understand your needs, and some training so that they are following your processes and systems (remember them?).

You can outsource things like: your bookkeeping, writing daily emails, newsletters and sales copy, managing your ads on Facebook, recruitment of staff, staff training, the list is endless. Of course, you will want to make sure you understand how to do all of these things so that you know you are getting quality work, and you have full control over what is delivered. But why do everything yourself if there are experts who can do it for you, in a timely manner so that you can get on with making your business grow?

Why wouldn't you want to outsource? Because it costs money. But consider that to make money you need to invest in things that are going to give you a return on your investment. If paying for someone to write your Facebook ads is going to cost you £250 a month, for example, and those ads bring you in five new clients a week, and they have a lifetime value of £1000 per year, is a £3000 spend per year worth £250,000 return? Even if the lifetime value of a client is half that, or the number of new clients is fewer, what makes more sense? Only you can decide what is going to make the best ROI, but I suggest you outsource the things you can't do, won't do, or just really hate doing but need to be done to keep the business running.

## Delegate

There will be staff you can trust with everything and staff that are just there to do the thing they are good at. With the staff you can trust with everything, delegate them with more work or responsibility. You don't have to compensate them monetarily, some staff work better with recognition and status rather than a higher wage. Delegating jobs like proof-reading to a competent receptionist, or writing up processes to a keen senior who is looking to operate her own business one day, takes the load off you.

Delegate tasks that take up 80% of your time and only give you 20% of your return. Make a list of all the things that are necessary to be done but not necessarily done by you and can be delegated. Delegation leads to staff buy-in as well. If staff can see what you are doing in the business and not only why it is important, but also be involved in delivering it, they will have a better understanding of what you are trying to achieve. They may also have more pride in their work and be a more loyal staff member when they are tasked with 'being part of the business and making the business work' rather than just being an employee.

---

Why wouldn't you want to delegate? Because you're a control freak. Let it go.

---

With proper training and support for an intensive time, people will get it. It might not be 100% the way you would do it, but often they come up with an even better way, and done is usually good enough, if it leaves you time to concentrate on the priority tasks of growing your business.

## Automate

Computers may be the bane of your life, smartphones run your life, and tablets kill your life, but, used properly, they can help give you more time to do the important stuff. If you don't have a computer reservation system that tracks client details, services and spend and allows you to run reports to that effect, you should seriously consider getting one. I've seen salons that still operate on a diary and card system. It's not necessary, it's clunky, it's slow and you are missing out on a goldmine of knowledge and marketing. Autoresponders such as *Ontraport, Active Campaign, Infusionsoft* and *Aweber* allow you to set up a series of emails that will be served up automatically to clients who request them. This can be daily for a period of time or whatever frequency you need. Once it is set up it runs continuously until you tell it to stop.

> There is so much technology available to you in the way of automation, it's clever and can be intuitive.

### Why wouldn't you automate?

It takes a bit of work to set up some systems. And learning a new system can be a bore and a chore. And for some staff it can be scary. Strap on a pair and get it done. Automation is usually done once, runs along happily in the background and gives you more time to do what you want.

## Your Productivity

So let's be brutally honest. How productive do you think you really are? Here's an exercise in accountability:

First you are going to look at how you currently use your time. This bit will take a bit of work, it's not a quick fix, so you have to be fully committed to it. And you have to be honest. OK so far?

So, take a piece of paper (you could also do this on a tablet if you prefer) and down the side mark out time in half hour blocks. Start at the time you wake up, e.g., 6.30am and mark from there 7.00am, 7.30am, 8.00am, etc. until you get to the time you go to bed. This is just for one day.

Starting on the day you are going to undertake this task, write down everything you have done in that half hour.

**So it might look something like this:**

6.00am - Alarm, woke, checked Facebook and personal emails.

6.30am - Showered and dressed for work.

7.00am - Got kids up.

7.30am - Breakfast and school lunches made.

And keep going until the end of the day when you close your eyes to go to sleep.

You can repeat this for another day if you wish, but for a 24-hour period you should be getting quite a clear picture of what you actually do all day. (And no, you don't have to share this with anyone else.) The results will probably surprise you.

When I did this myself with a group of people it was amazing how much time we spent on Facebook, surfing the net, making cups of coffee, and so on. And what was a really 'busy' day ended up being not that productive at all.

Now put that information into the following matrix, from Stephen Covey's *'The 7 Habits of Highly Successful People.'*

This matrix is a scale for urgent and important tasks. The two of which are very different animals and are often confused. You can have important tasks, which are not urgent, but if you don't do them become so. And you can have urgent tasks that are not necessarily important in that the goal of driving your business forward is not governed by them.

|  | Urgent | Non-Urgent |
|---|---|---|
| **Important** | Q1 | Q2 |
| **Not Important** | Q3 | Q4 |

*Figure 3. Stephen Covey's Time-Management Matrix*

At the top of the vertical (Y) axis we have tasks that are important, going down the scale to tasks that are unimportant. Along the horizontal (x) axis are the tasks from urgent to non-urgent.

**The matrix gives us 4 quadrants:**

**Q1: Are tasks that are both urgent and important.** These can be crisis situations, like the boiler blowing up leaving you with no hot water and therefore no service; urgent problems, like the VAT return not been done and the deadline is tomorrow; or project deadlines, this book publishing deadline being in two weeks and I still need to complete 20,000 words.

**Q2: Are the tasks that are not urgent but important to the business being driven forward.** This can be things like preparation of copy for a landing page, strategic planning of the next 12 months, and building client relationships with daily emails and newsletters.

**Q3: Are the tasks that are urgent but not important.** These include interruptions by others, some phone calls, most emails, meeting other people's expectations and priorities rather than your own.

**Q4: Are the tasks that are not urgent and non-important and include**: some phone calls and emails, checking Facebook posts, idly surfing the internet, watching TV and most other leisure activities. (There is a place for leisure activities but not when you are on task and growing your business.)

Which quadrant did the majority of your activities over the last day or two fit into? I would hazard a guess that your matrix is skewed towards Q3 and Q4. So, in order to make the change you need to move towards a more efficient you and a more profitable business, here's what you need to do:

*Manage* all the tasks in Q1. If they are there you haven't

managed to prevent them becoming both urgent and important. Some of these things are non-preventable, but for example, was the boiler serviced on time?, was the VAT return outsourced and the information sent as it happened rather than at the last minute? What systems can you put in place so that the important stuff is done so it doesn't become urgent? What things can be automated?

*Focus your attention* on tasks in Q2. These activities are what will drive your business forward, get you closer to your goals and take away the hassle in your life. Spend most of your time here; the top 20% of these activities will bring in 80% of your profits.

*Use caution* with the tasks in Q3. You can eliminate a lot of the unnecessary interruptions by careful training of staff and delegating tasks. Reservation system down? Don't deal with it yourself, train all the staff to know who to call to fix it. Outsource the bigger headaches and empower people to take responsibility and get on with the job.

*Avoid* all tasks in Q4. If you want your business to succeed, you need to change the habit of watching TV after your evening meal and instead plan a loyalty system for your top clients. Turn off Facebook, turn off Twitter, turn off the internet if you have to. We are easily distracted by bright, shiny things and the norm is to take the easy route. Watching TV is easy. Checking Facebook every 10 minutes is easy. Writing a sales letter is work. I did tell you this was going to be work, didn't I? But watching TV is not going to get you new clients through the door. Checking Facebook posts will not help you retain your current clients.

Writing down your day like this once you make changes helps you to change your habits and cement them in place.

Research with hip-replacement patients in Scotland showed that the ones who kept a written diary about their recovery and their goals for exercise each day, actually recovered almost three times more quickly than those who just thought about it (read more about this study in 'The Power of Habit,' by Charles Duhigg).

Just thinking about it and saying to yourself, *"I'm going to do it,"* usually doesn't turn into actions. Writing things down, however, makes you more committed to taking action, and gives you a visual cue of what action you need to take.

## Dealing with distractions

Bright and shiny things are dangled in your way every day. Particularly in the hair and beauty industry. And you are not unlike the 100% of other humans on the planet that are distracted by them. There are ways to avoid them, but most of the time you want to minimise them to focus on the more important task of working towards your goals. This is a big topic and there are many resources out there to help you, the key is to find the right ones for you, and use them. Here's some that I find really useful:

### Website blockers

I have an app called Anti-Social installed on my computer and my iPhone to block websites I know I get distracted by during my day. This allows me to block all websites without having to turn off the internet, or I can select specific sites that I want to turn off, and for what period of time. It catches me every time. When I think I'm being efficient and focused and I flick to Hotmail, for example, I get the message that I can't access it and it gives me a kick up the arse and I'm back on task. None of us are infallible and we all need reminders.

### Get out of your environment

When I was working from home in London I would be constantly *"I just have to... put another load of washing on,"* or *"I just have to...tidy up the kitchen,"* or *"I just have to... etc.."*. In order to get out of that environment and into somewhere more productive I joined a private members' club. Sounds posh but the monthly fees were no more than joining a gym. It gave me space away from all the *'just having to...'* distractions and somewhere I felt I could go to just work. It was a great place to network too and over time, I picked up a number of clients and suppliers as well.

### Get off the floor

If you are still working *in* your business and have no time to work *on* your business, get off the floor. Reduce the number of days you are 'face to face' with clients by one. If you have the systems and procedures in place you will not be missed by staff and the business will carry on without you. In fact, it may even do better without you. Use that one day to focus on making the business more profitable; all the tasks in Q2 of the matrix on page 203. Then take another day out of the salon so you are working two days on the business, and so on.

## Real Life Example

This works, I know because I did this with Terry. It was uncomfortable for him at the start as he thought he would lose business but it worked for many reasons. The first was that I could have his undivided attention to plan, create, write for and grow the business at least one full day per week. He would also come to the club with me so that we were both in 'work mode'. The second was it gave the staff more autonomy to run the business. Systems and procedures were written down and everyone was trained on them so that they knew what to do.

We promoted one staff member to be a 'day manager' on the days that Terry was out of the salon. That 'day manager' was responsible for the general running of the salon and they were compensated financially and gained recognition and status from the rest of the team. The team did their jobs better because we trusted them to do so. Terry's clients became even more loyal to him, as he was on the floor less; his appointments were harder to come by. Creating scarcity like this helped us to raise his prices and created urgency for his clients to book far in advance.

## Schedule your time

In the marketing mastermind group I am part of, there was a bit of a flurry of excitement over a technique of getting more done in your day by getting up earlier. The proponent of the technique - Den - advocated getting out of bed every morning at 5am so that you had more hours in your day and could be more productive. There were other aspects to it, like doing it for 66 days to set the new behaviour as a habit and such like, but for now I'll stick to the 5am starts. You can imagine the furore in the group as each stated their personal preference for sleeping hours – *"Early morning, always have been"; "Late morning, can't face the sunrise"; "You've got to be joking!"; "I'll give it a go but it will kill me,"* and so on.

Everyone was different and didn't believe that changing a waking habit would get the results (the claim was that you would be 95% more productive), they were correct in a way, but not because of their skepticism. A few said they would try the 5am starts and see if it worked. I wasn't sure of Den's claims either, as since having a child who is an early riser, and a schedule that means we all have to be out of the house by 6.30, I'm forced to start my day early. But then he explained a bit more about it, and it wasn't the getting up at 5am that was the key. The key was the scheduling of tasks throughout his day. See figure 4 for his schedule. (Copied with permission.)

*Figure 4. Den's Schedule*

The habit was to change the way he structured his day, and putting formal times in place to work on each area that needed to be done.

My mentor, Jon, does something similar, and also uses an app to structure his day in further detail. It's called the Pomodoro Technique, which I have explained in detail later in the chapter, but in a nutshell it segments your working times into 25 minute lots (called Pomodoros), with breaks between them.

**Jon also gave me the benefit of his Typical Daily Routine, which goes along the lines of:**

7.00am - Get up and work at the kitchen table

9.00am to 11.00am - Cycling, 20 miles

11.00am - 12.00pm - Work in Cave (his office)

12.00pm - Pre-workout breakfast

1.00pm - 1.40pm - Nap

2.00pm - 3.30pm - Workout

4.00pm - 7.00pm - Work in Cave

7.00pm - Dinner

7.30pm - 9.00pm - Work in Cave

9.00pm to whenever - Chill

Initially when I saw this it made me laugh - a lot. I love Jon, he's one of the most successful, intelligent, creative, filthy, and for an old man, fit person I know. He has a unique way of thinking called 'double-tracking' like me (a subject for another book). He's me, just older, balder and has a dick. But that's not what's funny. When I look at schedules like this, it bears no resemblance to my day at all. I sometimes think that men have it all that much easier when they write shit like this because they generally aren't responsible for running a household as well as everyone's social life and their own business. I'm not complaining, I love being a woman and would rather be a woman knowing what I know than a man who is led by his stomach and his dick. But that's another story. What I am trying to show you is that you can still do the work required to do when you schedule proper time for it and make it a habit.

**Here's my typical day (days vary with different activities but it's the general rule for me to be as productive as I can):**

5.15am - Get up, wake the child up

5.45am - Breakfast, get the child ready for school

6.30am - School run

7.30am - 8.30am - Exercise (Gym or run)

8.30am – 9.00am - Shower and schedule the day

9.00am - 12.00pm - Work in office

12.00pm - 12.30pm - Lunch

12.30pm - 1.30pm - School run

2.00pm - 6.00pm - After school activities, help with homework, household chores

6.00pm - 7.00pm - Dinner

7.00pm - 9.00pm - Work in office

9.00pm - Bed

My scheduled work time is reduced to five hours per day, as opposed to seven and a half hours that Jon has. And what I haven't really shown here is how much time is taken up planning, cajoling, driving, motivating, organising, mediating, negotiating, feeding, consoling, running around for one child, one husband and a small fluffy white cat, so that each one is happy and not giving me grief.

What I also don't show here is when I am out at the beach or by the pool watching sailing or swimming lessons, I also take a book and a pencil and write, plan and list. I'm one of those unapproachable mums who likes to be on her own in a corner and not be disturbed by talking.

It's worked for me so far and I manage to get as much, if not more, done this way.

To be fair to Jon, he also has a role to play with family and his example was to show that his day is based on routine, as is every successful person's. The fact is, he has a routine and it is set in stone. His routine is planned and structured and that means he gets stuff done.

My point is: create your own schedule, stick to it, and make it a habit.

### Work out your top 20%

When you have shut yourself away and have your schedule, you want to spend 80% of your time working on the top 20% of your business that is going to make the most money. I spend the first 20 minutes of my work schedule writing my daily email. That is one of the most important tasks in my business, as it is the one that makes me the most money. So I do it every day. It's a no-brainer, but it means that I'm not going to spend time looking at Facebook and responding to posts, or liking things so that it looks as if I give a shit and am engaging with people. There is no money to be made there, so it's not in my top 20%; it's not even in my top 80% to be fair.

In my salon, one of the biggest sources of income, next to daily emails, was referrals. So again, I would spend time testing, measuring and tweaking our referral process. It was important to get it right as it made us money - every day, and the ROI on this was out of this world. It made sense to be doing that and not tweeting something inane to the world, or retweeting someone else's opinions. That stuff can be done - for fun - but not at the expense of the stuff that is going to keep you in business.

You will probably have a feeling about what things are working in your business already and what you need to focus on.

But going back to your strategy - getting good clients in and keeping them there - make sure you are working on things that you can measure, replicate and scale. Facebook 'likes' might be ego boosting but they don't mean sales. Instagram gives you a platform for your pretty pictures but you can't reliably measure clients in the door from a picture. SEO is cheap but you can't replicate it or scale it up to do more of it, making you money.

### Pomodoro technique

This simple app is a great way to keep you accountable to time. I have used it in the writing of this book, as, like most people, I struggle at times to keep to a task. My mind flits all over the place, and when I think I have sat at my desk and written for a solid hour, in reality, I will have written for five minutes, thought about something unrelated for 10 minutes, gone and got a cup of tea for another 10 minutes, as I also loaded the dishwasher, returned to the office and looked at the computer, written for five minutes, heard the washing machine finish, put the washing in the dryer, got another load of laundry on, gone to the toilet, come back to my desk, written for five minutes and shit... one hour has gone by. And guess what? I have only written for 15 minutes out of the 60 and wonder why I am not getting much done.

But then the Pomodoro app came along my path and it all changed. The way it works is that you set a timer or a 'pomodoro' (Italian for tomato and named after a tomato-shaped kitchen timer by its inventor Francesco Cirillo) for a number of minutes.

**There are 6 steps to the principle:**

1. Decide on the task to be done.

2. Set the pomodoro timer to n minutes (traditionally n = 25)

3. Work on the task until the timer rings. If a distraction pops into your head, write it down, but immediately get back on task.

4. After the timer rings, take a short break of five minutes.

5. Go back to step one and repeat for four pomodoros.

6. After four pomodoros, take a longer break (15–30 minutes), and repeat from step one until the task is complete.

The app will automate all of this for you including the breaks and the number of pomodoros to be achieved. I have the app on my phone and can see the countdown out of the corner of my eye, which spurs me on to write faster and for a more consistent period.

### Work in your optimal time

Many things in your life are determined by the clock: getting out of bed, your first appointment of the day, what time school finishes and when you have to collect the children. But your creativity is not necessarily determined so. I found this out a while ago, and I am more creative and more alert in the afternoon. So for me, it makes more sense to do the creative things like designing an advert or writing a landing page at around 3pm. I'm more focused on analytical things, such as invoicing and analysing results early in the morning after I have exercised.

And this may be just a habit, but every morning I churn out the list of things I need to achieve that day and do the important things that need an analytical mind in the morning and the more creative things in the afternoon. I also find that once my morning tasks are finished, I have a clear mind and am not being distracted by what needs to be done.

### Train the immediate people in your life

I had a problem with being available for my little family all of the time. As a mum and wife, I feel the guilt of not being there all the time if I think my family needs me. When I'm working, there is always a nag in the back of my head that I should be doing something for them. I can't stop it, it's part of my make-up, but I can manage it. First I had to make the decision that to enjoy the freedom I have to do the things I want, I have to commit to making my business work. That means sacrificing some time with my family.

I have to admit that I have a very supportive husband. Mr QBofE is a very patient guy and he knows how important my work is. As my daughter gets older and more independent, I spend less time helping her physically, and more time letting her do her own creative thing. But they both know that when my office door is closed, unless there is a fire or flood, they are not to come in. Although I have had less success training the cat to stop meowing at a closed door - there's one creature who knows the true meaning of relentless.

One of my colleagues in my marketing mastermind group has three closed doors between herself and the rest of her staff in the office. Each door has a note on it starting with, *"Have you tried to come up with the solution to your problem first?"* through to indicating that your interruption better be a national emergency before you even consider knocking on the last door. It's helped her reduce her interruptions to almost zero and has made the staff take responsibility for doing the job they've been trained to do, as well as using their brains.

> Just like your clients, you need to train the people in your life that you are available only when you say so.

It's a non-compromising situation and when you are seeing the rewards you all share in those together.

### Exercise

This may sound like an odd tactic but if I miss my daily morning session in the gym or a swim, I do not perform as well as I could. It's not at all surprising though. Repetitive exercise (like cycling or swimming laps) stimulates brain waves that are associated with creativity, vivid imagery and learning. Some of your best business ideas will come to you when you are exercising. Exercise also makes the body release neurotransmitters responsible for boosting your mood and, even more exciting, studies are starting to show the link between exercise and repair of brain neurons and prevention of brain 'shrinkage'.

Exercising is also a 'Gateway' or 'Keystone Habit' as described by Charles Duhigg in his book *'The Power of Habit.'* These habits are the ones that other good habits are linked to and become a system. The habit of exercise promotes the habit of healthy eating and the habit of good sleep, and so on, because of the impact exercise has.

### Diarise and list

Create a list of all the things you need to do each morning, order them into the things that are most productive to making money for your business, and give the highest priority to those that are important and going to get you to your goals. Cross off the tasks on the list as you complete them. This gives you a visual way of tracking your productivity.

### Write off days

I'm not a machine and I'm not going to admit that every day is a successful, done-everything-I-wanted-to-achieve day. There are days when nothing goes right when I feel like I am pushing shit uphill. With a rake. I call them 'write off days'. But coming back to my old friend the 80/20 Principle it's OK. If I am relentless and set the time and actually sit down and focus every day, 80% of the stuff will get done. And that's probably 79% more than anybody else, ipso facto, I am going to achieve more.

It's like fitness and weight loss. Change happens gradually over a period of time. If you set out to get fit and lose weight, it's going to happen incrementally over the time that you put the effort in, and by scheduling in the programme every day. If you miss a day that's fine, if you miss consecutive days, you start to lose what you achieved, but if you miss weeks you've got a shit show. Don't beat yourself up if one day it doesn't all go to plan. But start going Cassius Clay on your arse if you don't do anything at all.

Getting things done is not due to lack of ideas or knowledge. There is plenty of information and compelling evidence out there to help you achieve better business success. The reason that you will fall down on putting this knowledge into place, including all the information in this book, is due to you not acting on it. It's not only the lack of implementation but also the lack of consistency. When you set goals at the start of your year for your business, or you get all motivated after reading this book, you get all excited and have a flurry of activity. And then the 12 months of your year yawns out like a gaping chasm, things get in the way and you put things off. By the time the end of the year comes around you are either busy trying to get things done as fast as you can and failing, or you have given up with a defeatist shrug of the shoulders and said it was too hard anyway.

---

## *Advanced Bonus: The 12 Week Year*

---

Well, if you are serious about implementation and being accountable you should consider joining my Inner Circle, but more about that at the end of this book. You can also take advantage of the system called the *'The 12 Week Year'* devised by Brian Moran and Michael Lennington, which they explain in their book aptly titled, *'The 12 Week Year: Get More Done in 12 Weeks Than Others do in 12 Months.'* The 12 Week Year is a system that turns your 12-month year into a cycle that is only 12 weeks long. It redefines your year for you and makes you concentrate on the important things and the priorities that will actually bring you money through the door. It creates an urgency to do the things that matter the most and helps you keep track. If you are at all serious about getting stuff done, this system will improve your productivity by at least 30%.

### Getting buy-in from your team

These strategies and tactics are all well and good, and if done correctly, will make you a shitload of money. But I will tell you now, like anything new you are going to come up against a lot of resistance from your team (you may even come up against resistance from your friends, family and even partner too, which sounds odd, but it happens). If you are going to implement, say, for example, daily emails, you will have your staff telling you that they wouldn't want to receive an email every day, so why should the clients. Your stylist will say, *"But what if I lose a client because they get sick of the emails?"* The list will go on, and there will be rumblings behind your back. At this point you will want to cheerfully sack the lot of them, or at least ask, *"Who the hell owns this business anyway?!"*

The best way to get team buy in is to a) educate them in why you are doing what you are doing, and b) give them some responsibility in the process.

---

Educating staff is always difficult if they don't see what is in it for them.

---

You need to present what you are going to do in order to get more of the right clients through the door, or getting more out of your current clients, in a way that the staff see the short and long-term benefits for themselves. You want to tell them that with the new strategy of targeting your ideal clients, they will get clients they like to deal with, who don't quibble over prices and are going to be more loyal. Guaranteeing them a better working environment, better commissions and more of a certain future with your business. When they start to get a bit anxious about not accepting certain types of clients, you go back to the strategy that not all clients are created equal, the more you have to deal with the hard to please price-buying client, the less you will enjoy your job.

Would you rather! Would you rather!

**Would you rather:**

A salon of loyal clients you like and will do what you say in regards to their haircare because they trust you and pay you well?

*Or...*

A column of walk-ins who query the price before you start and whom you never see again because they are chasing the next 'bargain', constantly having to deal with shitty hair because they care more about the price rather than the long-term goal of healthy hair?

Educating staff will be like educating clients. It is a constant process and even if you think they get it, they will still come back with the same fears because they are not you and not the one in charge of the business. They will only ever see it from their own perspective. Although, the day you hear a 21-year old stylist tell a client in her first consultation that she could not possibly be a client of the salon because her demands for her hair are not in line with the practices of the salon, is a very proud moment and worth the constant reinforcing of what it is you want to achieve.

Present your ideas and strategies to the team at your weekly meeting instead of going over the same old *"put the colours away after use,"* or, *"clean the basin between each client"*. Get their thoughts, but only for your benefit of overcoming the objections, and print off your ideal client avatar and display it prominently in the back room. And buy them all a copy of this book as a present, and make them read it!

Giving responsibility in some of the processes is a bit easier than the education. When I announced that I was going to start email marketing the QBofE way to the team, and said I was going to be sending daily emails to all the clients in the system, I got a mixed response. I knew it would be contentious because anything out of the ordinary can and will be uncomfortable for people to accept - even if you are paying their wages.

My concern was the rumblings from the reception team that

they wouldn't want to receive a daily email, so our clients wouldn't either. *"That's right,"* I explained. *"Nobody wants to receive a boring email that is trying to hard sell them something every day, but they will like the emails I'm going to send and we need to test it and give it a chance."*

My main concern was that the reception is the main point for collecting email addresses from clients coming into the salon. They were the ones who were trained to get the client details, and if they were not buying-in to my marketing tactic then they would fail to get the addresses because of their own preconceived ideas. So I took the route of getting the reception team to proof read my draft email before it went out. I would write it in the morning, get them to proof-read it and queue it up for the afternoon delivery through the automated system. It didn't take long for them to see that the emails were entertaining and useful and then start seeing the responses from the clients.

Once the initial shedding of unsubscribers finished they were getting delighted comments from clients when checking in or checking out, and it gave them something else to connect with the client. They became very motivated to get the correct email address after that and stressed to the client that they would enjoy their daily dose of email. And of course, once the book *'101 Naked Confessions of a Gay Hairdresser,'* taken from the top emails of the year, was published, they had more motivation to get clients to hand over their details. This one small step of proof-reading opened up more acceptance and uptake of any other tactics I tested.

Even if they did roll their eyes and say, *"here she goes again..."*!

## Remember: Relentless

The overall premise to getting stuff done is to make the decision that you want to. Without this, nothing is going to change for you. And when it works don't stop, do more.

Lather, rinse, repeat.

## Chapter 14. Summary

→ **Just Fucking Do It**. None of this information will be any good to you if you don't use it and implement the strategy in your business.

→ **Give yourself more time by outsourcing, delegating and automating everything you can.**

→ **Focus on the non-urgent, important tasks that move your business forward.** Manage the urgent, important tasks and let the rest take a back seat.

→ **Remove distractions from your business and life, so that you can spend time doing what you need to do to make your business succeed.**

→ **Get buy-in from your team by educating them in your strategy and the tactics you will be using to build the business.** Allow them to be involved in some way so that they give you their full support.

→ **Be relentless.**

### Take Action

Create a routine. Work out the top 20% most productive things you can do for your business growth, and make them a priority in your routine. Bite the bullet and outsource, delegate or automate all the rest.

# CHAPTER FIFTEEN
# PUTTING IT ALL TOGETHER

When I worked for an antipodean travel company we would have a session with our team once a year where we wrote up a BOF. A *Brightness Of Future*. Sounds woo, and it is a little bit but the reasoning behind it was sound. In order to achieve anything, you have to have a goal or target with a desired outcome, a strategy to go about it, and the knowledge of what to put into place to do it. The BOF we had to write was a 10-year vision of not only what we ourselves would have achieved, but also what the company would look like.

The goal of a BOF wasn't to write a serious *"I will have earned 30K per year and paid off my loans,"* it was required to be a fantastical look at where you would be in 10 years time. Nothing was limited; your imagination could work overtime. If you could see the company providing you with flying cars to get to and from work, you wrote it down. If you saw yourself on a beach on a private island working three hours a day remotely, you wrote it down.

Nothing was too stupid, too outrageous, too extravagant. It was a bit of fun, but it served two purposes: 1. A lot of what the company implemented over the years came from these BOFs. Some of the ideas people wrote down weren't that far-fetched or unreasonable, and it gave the bosses information on what would make the staff happy and more productive. 2. When you have no restrictions on what you should be doing in your business, or thinking about your goals, you overcome your own self-limiting beliefs. It stops you from getting in your own way.

Usually the restrictions we think are in place to becoming successful are self-imposed. Generally from what we think other people in the industry, or friends and family think of us. It doesn't make any sense, right? Why should we not do something because of our own fear about what someone else might think? So before you start conquering your niche, get yourself into the mindset that *you can do this.* It's not hard. It does require work. But the rewards are worth it.

**Here's a simple question for you:**

*If you woke up tomorrow and your business was perfect, what would it look like?*

Hopefully you should now be motivated to get stuck in and make what I have shown you work. And to help you, I've asked some questions below to stimulate your thinking about your business and where you want it to go. If you can answer each of these in detail, and be completely honest with yourself, you will be surprised how easy it will be to take the steps you need to *Grow Your Salon FAST.* Decide what you want. If you don't, there is no point to any of this.

**And one last thing - write the answers down.**

→ What do you want to be doing?

→ With whom?

→ What do you need to achieve it?

*Using the 80/20 Principle:*

→ What is making you the most money?

→ Who are your best clients?

→ What are you selling?

→ To whom do you want to sell it?

→ What or who is causing you the biggest hassles?

→ Why should people buy from you rather than others in your industry?

→ Do you actually have a competitor?

→ What's the lifetime value of your clients?

→ How much are you prepared to pay for a new one?

→ Where are the people you want to sell to?

→ Where are they looking and what defines them?

→ How can you get your message in front of them?

→ How much more or what else can you sell them?

→ What experience do they have throughout your sales process?

When I was doing a bit of research for this book, I came across an interview I did for a marketing newsletter of one of the biggest DRM names in the UK. I was asked what I was doing in terms of DRM and after a long-winded answer of all the tactics, I said, *"What I have learned is to do as much as possible. It doesn't matter how good it is. Just do it. Do everything at once."* The King of Direct Response Marketing, and multiple author on the subject, Dan Kennedy, says that when you are marketing your business, *"Sling mud at the wall and see if some of it sticks."*

Getting things done means it doesn't have to be perfect, good enough is good enough. If it's sitting on your desk waiting to be perfected it is making far less sales than if it is published with it being not quite right. So get it out there and then tweak it based on the response. But don't just sling any old mud at the walls. Have a strategy, and bear in mind the overall purpose of your marketing: Making money and growing your salon.

## Sometimes pretty pictures work best

I have a science background. But that's not important. I've heard marketing systems described in many ways, but given my background, here is my take on it. It's the best way I could think of for creating a visual that summed up the system. And being in the industry you are in - you deal with chemistry every day. Don't tell me you don't; getting the right mix of developer to bleach and the chemical change in hair when you apply colour is your area of expertise. If it's not, put this book down. Your business is suffering from something much more serious than a lack of marketing. I'm serious.

Anyway, I would like to introduce you to *The Funnel/Flask System*. Or FFS for short. (Please see diagram on opposite page.)

## FFS

Your leads are sitting in there in the 5ltr container - your market - waiting to be poured into your funnel. They are in that container and have come from the ads you are putting on and in Facebook, LinkedIn, newspapers, radio, referrals, magazines, YouTube, Google, direct mail, etc. From these sources they pour into your funnel and start the chemical change of transformational selling and relationship building. Even though these leads are highly qualified through your targeted ads, there is a filter paper in place to stop the chavs, peasants and commoners slipping through any further. This is through your positioning at the start of your nurturing campaign.

The leads progress through the neck of the funnel where they receive your email sequence or are qualified with a phone consultation, leading to a face-to-face consultation. Or a combination of the above. They buy your initial product or service and become a client.

They have entered the flask.

The beauty of this flask is it's designed to be swirled or stirred without losing any of its contents. You have a captured audience, and what you do with them after that first purchase is crucial to keeping them as a repeat client.

Having said that, there is a gap between the end of the funnel

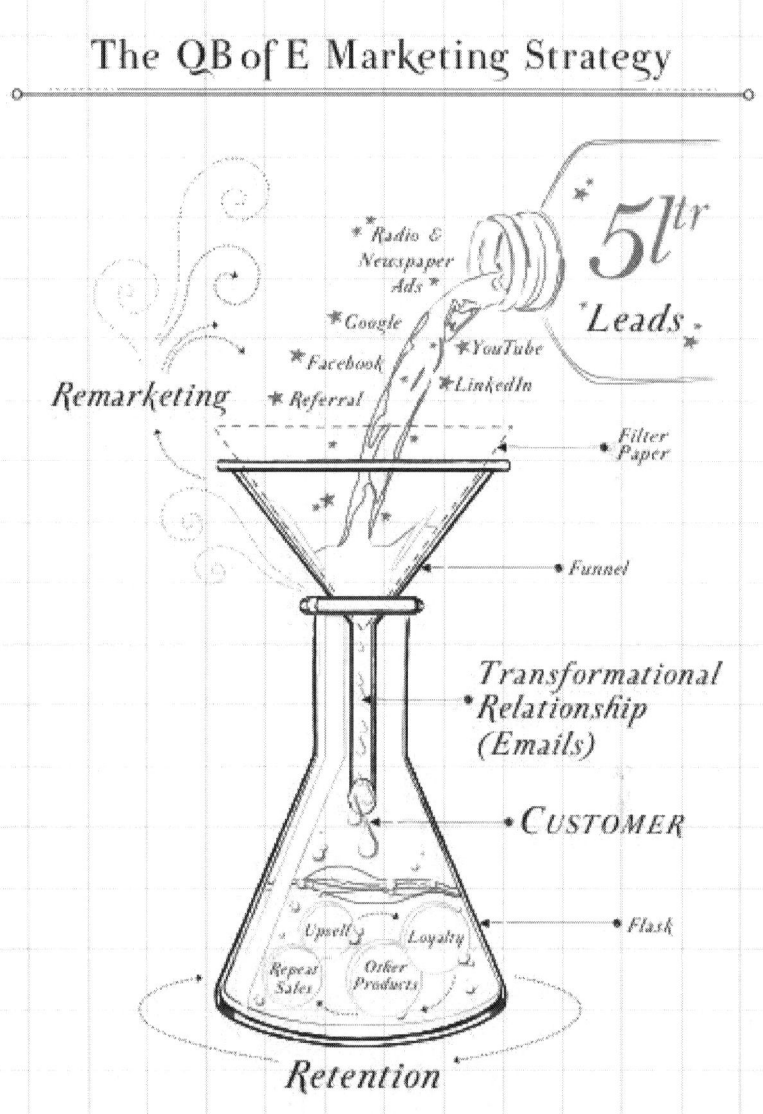

*Figure 5. The Funnel Flask System.*
*From generating new leads, through to being a loyal customer*

and the flask, where leads who are not ready to buy from you yet can escape, and then be hit with remarketing campaigns until they die, buy or fly (unsubscribe).

Once you have your clients buying from you in your flask, it is in your best interest to keep them there. And if they are getting value from you, it is in their best interest too. You can sell different products or services to them (upsells), more of the same product or services (repeats) more often. You swirl and nurture and create serial clients.

## Chapter 15. Summary

→ **The restrictions you think are in place that will stop you becoming successful are self-imposed.** Fear is what holds you back.

→ **This chapter gives you the marketing system you can follow, from lead generation through to follow up.** It is a simple system and gives you all you need to Grow Your Salon FAST.

### Take Action

Answer the question: *"If you woke up tomorrow and your business was perfect, what would it look like?"*

# CHAPTER SIXTEEN
# CONCLUSION - LET'S GET STARTED

You've now read what I have to say, seen the examples and the results. Now it's your turn. I'm not going to leave you high and dry and say that's it. That's not in my nature. I would genuinely like to see your business succeed, using the strategies I have shown you and the reasons behind them.

At the back of this book there is an invitation to join my inner circle, where you will get support, information and personalised advice in the form of critiques.

But it's not for everyone, so have a good think about what you want to achieve in your business in the next 12 months. If you want to remain with the status quo, what you have read in this book will not hurt you. If you want to grow and make more profit, reading this book is fine, but now you have to implement what you have learnt.

I have given you a lot of information and it's hard to know where to start, so I'm going to be a nice Queen Bitch and give you a head start.

**Here's your strategy:**

- Choose a message to resonate with your target market - think: *why should they buy from me and no one else?*
- Choose the medium you are going to use to send the message.
- Begin the relationship by giving them something of high perceived value. (A book or report.)
- Follow up relentlessly.

**You might want to start like this:**

1.  **Analyse your market and create your Avatar.** This should be a nice creative exercise and you can do it away from the business. Book a day in a hotel room or in a posh coffee shop, or wherever you feel most creative and have no distractions from staff, family, or washing machines.

2.  **Website.** Create/overhaul your website so that it meets the criteria for DRM. Each page does one thing. Capture your leads with opt-ins.

3.  **Autoresponder.** Write the sequence of emails that your leads are going to automatically receive when they opt-in from your website or landing pages.

4.  **Start writing daily emails to your existing clients so you are front of mind when they need you.**

5.  **Advertise yourself on whatever platform you think your ideal client might be lurking.**

6.  **Follow up all those prospects who subscribe to your emails or download your report or buy your book.**

Simple.

JFDI.

## Chapter 16. Summary

Chapter 16 really is just a summary in and of itself. But what I would like you to do is take the strategy that you wrote in *Take Action, Chapter 1*, and compare it to the strategy you can put in place now that you know what you should be doing. How does it differ?

# APPENDIX I

## Copywriting Exercise

You may be like one of the many people I talk to, who say they cannot write. Surprisingly, most people are usually able to come up with something to write about, but get stuck in actually getting it down on paper.

I got this technique from my marketing mentor, Jon McCulloch, and I have done this exercise a number of times at various events he has hosted. It never fails to amuse me that in a room of hundreds of people who say they cannot write for shit, at the end of the exercise they have written something worth publishing.

### How to Write Like a Demon

Read through the exercise at least once before actually doing it.

1. **Get your kitchen timer or your phone, set it for five minutes and sit yourself down comfortably at your computer, ready to type.** Put the timer where you cannot see the countdown.

2. **Take three words at random.** For the purpose of this exercise, we're going to use cabbage, microphone and bucket. When we come to use this in anger, we'll choose our words more carefully.

3. **There are now two rules concerning these three words.**

   a. The first word of the first sentence must be any one of those three words.

   b. The other two words must then appear somewhere in the first sentence.

4. **OK, just read the three words again and then make sure you understand the two rules concerning them.**

5. **Now, set the timer going and start typing.** The rules for writing are:

   a. You write as fast as you can, just getting down whatever comes into your head in your 'stream of consciousness'.

   b. You do not edit, evaluate, or judge at this point. You write.

   c. You write from the instant you set the timer going and you don't stop until the timer goes off. This is why you put it where you can't see it.

   d. When the timer goes off, you stop.

   e. Go back and read what you've written. You may now also edit it.

6. **That's it.**

One thing that I can pretty much guarantee is going to amaze you is the quality of what you've written. Before you actually do this exercise, my guess is that you will be sceptical and expect nonsense. But I can guarantee that it won't be nonsense. You may have to edit it, but in true 80/20 style, 80% of the good stuff is there already – in just five minutes.

Now, repeat the exercise as many times as you feel you need to, just to prove writing this, well, wasn't just a fluke.

**Here are some ideas for the three words to start you off each time:**

1. Banana, ladle, desk

2. Dog, astronaut, window

3. Telephone, fish, saucepan

4. Doctor, door, bicycle

5. Bookcase, carpet, curtain

6. Car, pebble, gate

7.  Witch, chair, fire

8.  Water, pecan nut, hat

9.  President, paperclip, microphone

10. Mouse-mat, diary, receipt

Don't worry about these being 'nonsense words'.

Even though they are, you're going to find you write some pretty cool stuff, regardless.

And just imagine what you're going to be turning out with a little more direction and focus…

The golden rule of writing like this is to *write as you speak.* Don't get all pompous, technical or formal. There is a time for that, but this is not one of them. If you write like you speak, your prospects will relate to you more easily, and when they meet you they will feel like they know you already. And the relationship of trust is formed.

And one last thing – it is not all about you. It's about your lead. So write to them. After you have written your copy go through and change all the *"me", "I",* and *"my"* to *"you",* and *"yours".*

# APPENDIX II

## Writing The Book

**Writing a book takes time but it is really not that difficult. Here are 3 easy ways to write a book:**

1. **Take 90 or so of your best daily emails or blogs, top and tail them (take the 'Dear x' and the call to action out) and intersperse them with 10 top tips for your client about their haircare or beauty regime.** Write an introduction and a closing chapter (pointing the reader at more resources, products and services), give it an attention-giving title like *'101 Naked Confessions of a Gay Hairdresser'* (but not this one as it is already taken, obvs.).

   Simple.

2. **Take the top 10 most frequently asked questions your clients ask you, write up the questions and a detailed one-page answer for each one (a page is approximately 350 words), separating it into sections of what, why and how.** Now take the top 10 questions clients don't ask but should know, write up the detailed one-page answer for each question in sections of what, why and how. Write an introduction and a closing chapter (pointing the reader at more resources, products, and services).

   Simple.

3. **This one is a bit harder and there is a bit more work involved. Organise your book into logical topics and then write about the topics, answering the questions which? what? where? who? why? when? and how?** Once you've done that, go through it again and answer the same

questions, but this time in the negative (e.g., if you've written about, *"who is this for...?"*, write about, *"who is this not for...?"*) Write an introduction and a closing chapter (pointing the reader at more resources, products, and services).

Simple.

I said three but there is a fourth way... If you are clever, and want to invest your time in other areas and get your book out there faster, hire a ghostwriter/copywriter. There are many out there who will be able to take your idea and write it for you. Just remember that they need to be writing in your voice. The maxim 'write like you speak' should be taken heed of here. You are sure to find one that will fit your personality and style.

Simple.

If you are going to write a book, just start. Even if you were slow and committed to writing 2 pages a day - that's around 700 words - you will have a decent-sized tome ready in less than 2 months. And then you can add 'published author' to your list of accomplishments, cementing your expert status and creating an awesome lead magnet for your business.

***JFDI.***

# ACKNOWLEDGEMENTS

I would like to acknowledge a few people who have helped me get through this book - you are only as good as the people you hang out with...

Kelvin Smith, Mr QBofE, my best mate and my long-time husband, for putting up with me, encouraging me, and generally being a laid-back Kiwi bloke.

Heléna Smith, my daughter, who lets me leave home every now and then.

Jon McCulloch, EBG and BFF, for being brilliant and letting me swipe his brilliance.

My Elite buddies who are always there, kicking my arse.

Hair Organics Notting Hill, and all who sail in her, for teaching me how.

My friends in the desert, who make sense of the nonsense.

*Thank you.*

# REFERENCES

*'101 Naked Confessions of a Gay Hairdresser: Quick, Dirty, and Uncensored Secrets to Perfect Hair from the World's Most Outrageous Hairdresser,'* by Kat Smith and Terry Wilson

*'Build a Business from your Kitchen Table,'* by Sophie Cornish and Holly Tucker

*'Influence: The Power of Persuasion,'* by Robert Cialdini

*'Inside Her Pretty Little Head,'* by Jane Cunningham and Philippa Roberts

*'The 7 Habits of Highly Effective People,'* by Stephen Covey

*'The 80/20 Principle,'* by Richard Koch

*'The 12 Week Year: Get More Done in 12 Weeks than Others do in 12 Months,'* by Brian P Moran and Michael Lennington

*'Think and Grow Rich,'* by Napoleon Hill

*'Type & Layout: Are you Communicating or Just Making Pretty Shapes,'* by Colin Wheildon.

*'The Power of Habit,'* by Charles Duhigg.

*'Atlas Shrugged,'* by Ayn Rand

# AN EXCLUSIVE FREE GIFT FROM THE QBofE

'*Grow Your Salon FAST*' gives you everything you need to know to start, well, growing your salon fast. But I know you, because I am pretty sure you are like me and will want to see the hard evidence. Well, here is a free, exclusive gift for you. It's *'The GYSF Calculator To Better Profits'*. This clever little piece of kit will help you discover how much money you could be making if you implement the ideas and strategy in this book. It's very easy to do. You just enter some simple details, such as how often your clients visit you and how much you charge, and it will do the rest. I guarantee that you will be bowled over by the result. And it's not that hard. The default setting assumes a very conservative 20% uptake of more services and products, so imagine what will be possible when you really get stuck in.

**Go here to claim your free GYSF Calculator To Better Profits:**
*www.growyoursalonfast.com/gysfcalculator*

This is just my way of saying thank you for getting off your arse and being determined to succeed at growing your business.

# MORE ABOUT THE AUTHOR

By now you should know a little more about me from my writing, but here's the obligatory peek into my life...

I'm a Kiwi with an English mum and a Kiwi dad. I grew up in New Zealand, the Land of the Long White Cloud, went to Uni, got married, worked, and then moved to London, where I lived the dream for 13 years. For the past two and a half years I have been living the dream in the Middle East (and no, I am not going to tell you where in print as censorship and irrational emotional beliefs are alive and well here, even though it's the 21st century. And that's why we can't have nice things) with my husband, daughter and small, fluffy, white cat.

*'Grow Your Salon FAST'* is my second book. My first, *'101 Naked Confessions of a Gay Hairdresser'* was published in 2014 and was written over a very long, hot summer when everyone I knew had deserted the desert. I have written *'Grow Your Salon FAST'* as a blueprint for you to market your business successfully, because when I first owned a salon I was a bit lost. It took me a long time to work out what I needed to do. Although I did get some awesome expert help from the likes of Dan Kennedy, Chris Cardell and Jon McCulloch, I wish there had been something specifically tailored to salon owners at the time.

My goal for this book is to take the pain away from you having to start from scratch, so that you can focus on growing your salon with success.

I have private clients but at the moment my list is full and I very rarely open it up to new ones. The only way to access me would be to join my Inner Circle, which you can read more about here:

*www.growyoursalonfast.com/gysfinnercircle*

When I am not building my business I love the movies for pure escapism, a good book for the same reason, working out at the

242

gym and swimming, watching my daughter become a mini-QBofE, shopping for shoes and bling, drinking red wine, and travelling. I have been married by Elvis (truth) in Las Vegas, slept on a bed of ice and reindeer skins in Sweden, climbed a mountain in Borneo, had diarrhea and vomiting in the jungles of Burma, done aerobatics in a bi-plane in New Zealand and eaten donkey from a street stall in China.

Life is certainly not boring.